MW00827228

Vegetables for Carnivores

by

Greg Easter

FOREWORD

This is unlike any other book ever published. The original techniques and unexpected combinations of ingredients will enable you to replace meat in many recipes and produce rich, savory flavors from even the most bland of vegetables.

Dedicated to the pursuit of culinary advancement.

TABLE OF CONTENTS

INTRODUCTION

This book occasionally references the first three volumes of my **Cooking in Russia** book series and videos that you can find online at my YouTube channel:

www.youtube.com/user/cookinginrussia

Origin and Purpose

Several decades ago in Beverly Hills there was a grocery store called Mrs. Gooch's that had a large refrigerated case of unique vegetarian meals, some of which were along the lines of the recipes you will find in this book. These were sold in little plastic trays at a shockingly high price, but the customers there could afford them. I would get requests for foods like that fairly often from regulars at the hotel I worked at, as detailed in my book, *40 Years in One Night*. Some of the recipes that follow are from those days.

Instead of just handing you a collection of recipes to blindly follow, the purpose of this book is to explain the methodology and show how a dozen or so base preparations can be used to transmute many meat dishes into vegetarian delicacies.

Some of these recipes may seem daunting at first because they require you to cook ingredients before you even begin making your target dish. Bear in mind, these concentrated and seasoned vegetable preparations keep for a long time when refrigerated, so you can stock some of these up and use them when needed.

Vegetarian Cuisine vs. These Recipes

Anyone can produce a book of salad and soup recipes that will obey the rules of vegetarianism. Every bookstore has a dozen or more such titles. I have intentionally avoided such simple recipes here. These are recipes for the *reluctant* vegetarian—the person who is a carnivore at heart, but is compelled for whatever reason to try and switch to a plant based diet. It's not easy, but this will help a lot! These recipes will have you eating massive amounts of vegetables and your only complaint might be that they are more work to make than meat dishes. No argument there. Frying a burger up is far easier than any recipe here, but you can't have everything. If you want vegetables to taste like meat and satisfy you, it's going to take some work. Cows don't grow on trees. Although you might be able to fool your taste buds into thinking they do with some of the culinary trickery contained here.

Use of MSG

When it comes to making vegetable dishes resemble meat, the use of MSG is an invaluable tool. It is pure umami. I have repeatedly and emphatically denounced the notion that MSG is a harmful substance, but in case this is news to you, I will summarize the key points again here:

1. Monosodium Glutamate (MSG) is a naturally occurring substance in virtually every food you eat once it passes into your digestive system. The only difference between what you consume as protein and the MSG that may be added to a dish is that the latter is already broken down so that your tongue can taste it directly. To give you an idea of just how much MSG is naturally present in your food, take a look at the table on page 18 and note that even lentils contain 1.4 grams of MSG for every 100 grams, or 3.5 ounces (that's plain boiled with no seasoning added). If you think you can avoid MSG, you are grossly mistaken. Adding a half teaspoon of MSG to a pot of food means only a few milligrams will end up on your plate. This is enough to generate an umami (meat like) taste on your tongue, but truly microscopic in terms of the total intake you will have on any given day. If you could actually avoid MSG in your diet, such a diet would quickly kill you.

2. No double blind study has ever turned up someone who can tell the difference between MSG and a salt placebo. Food chemists jokingly call this phobia a form of psychosomatic hypochondria known as CRS, or *Chinese Restaurant Syndrome*. There is absolutely no scientific basis for having a reaction to a substance that is naturally present in your body and that you have been ingesting every day since *before* you were born! MSG is even in human breast milk. Beware: Medical doctors are not biochemists. Many go along with this fear mongering either to appease their patients, or simply

10

because they don't know any better. Again, a doctor is not a biochemist or a food scientist.

3. If you still aren't convinced, then ask yourself if you have a reaction to cheese, mushrooms, tomatoes and every single fast food menu item, because all of those things are extremely high in MSG. If you don't have a reaction to pizza or hot dogs, then you have just proven that you have no reaction to MSG.

4. The question some ask is why add it? For the same reason we add salt and pepper. Because it makes food taste better and a small amount does no harm. MSG is used by just about every famous chef, including Michelin star chefs. They just don't advertise it because they are aware of the public paranoia.

"Leaky Gut" Syndrome

Speaking of public fear and cashing in on pseudoscience, the Internet is the greatest boon to snake oil salesmen since the days of covered wagons and towns full of illiterate hayseeds. The first thing you need to accept (again) is that medical doctors are not biochemists by any stretch of the imagination. Medical students only have to pass the very most elementary chemistry and biochemistry classes in order to satisfy academic requirements. That's usually a single class—a few months a couple of times a week, even at top universities. A research biochemist will spend eight to ten years studying before he or she even enters the field. The sad fact is that the general public puts far too much trust and faith in the education of doctors. To the public, science is science, but it isn't. Medical science and biochemistry are two different fields. The idea that consuming legumes and grains will cause "leaky gut syndrome" is pure pseudoscience. Whatever you read about it online and in magazines is fear mongering, mostly designed to sell books and products. There is no credible scientific basis for such a thing. It's right up there with the fear of MSG.

Polyphenol Aftertaste

The methods used to boost or simulate meats and fish in this book largely rely on increasing the concentration of natural substances in foods, many of which are polyphenols. As explained in Volume 3 of the *Cooking in Russia* series, polyphenols have only weak tastes by themselves, but then can dramatically alter the way that we perceive other flavors. Some of these are slow to leave the palate. That is, once you eat something rich in polyphenols, the effect can linger for a long time after you are done eating that meal. This often leads to a delayed aftertastes that can be metallic or fishy, depending on many factors. Some people are much more prone to this than others. If you do experience this, you can clear your palate either with mouthwash or with hard liquor such as cognac or vodka. Beer and wine will *not* work, and can actually make the effect worse. It has to have a high alcohol content. Again, not everyone experiences this problem, though.

Measurement Conventions

While many cooks use terms like teaspoon and tablespoon very loosely, that is not how professional chefs operate. A teaspoon (abbreviated with a lower case t) is 5 cubic centimeters, or 5ml. A tablespoon (abbreviated as an upper case T) is 15 cubic centimeters, or 15ml, or 1/2 ounce. Careful measurement means reproducible results, and it is the path to perfecting any dish.

"Potato chips, iced tea and cupcakes are
a healthy lunch — it's vegetarian!"

APPROACH TO EATING

The classic *clockface* plating of meat, starch and vegetable doesn't apply to most of the recipes in this book, because there is no meat and a starch is often incorporated with the vegetables,

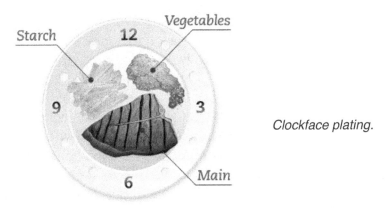

Clockface plating.

If you think about it, you'll realize that many great dishes combine a starch, vegetables and meat into a single item on the plate, such as lasagna or quiche. Just remember that the dishes here are already vegetables and starches, even when they don't look like it. You won't *need* to add side dishes, but it may help psychologically so that it seems like a complete meal for those who have been conditioned to think that way.

Psychological Satisfaction

One of the biggest problems that meat lovers have when trying to switch to a vegetarian diet is that it isn't satisfying in either flavor or in a sense of bulk. When you eat a big piece of meat, you will stay full for many hours. If you are used to that, then eating a plate of vegetables feels like you're still waiting for your meal to arrive. This is even more the case in today's world of industrialized farming where vegetables have very little flavor. They have been selectively bred and genetically modified so that they survive that long trip from the field to the processing plant, then to the warehouse where they sit, then on the truck heading to the local store's back room where they wait for space on a display to open up, and then to the store display where they wait for purchase, and then finally to your home where you just might stick them in your refrigerator for another week, and _still_ they look good! It doesn't matter if you buy them from a local farmer's market most of the time either, because they are still growing the same _type_ of fruits and vegetables that have been bred to survive the distribution method. Eating fresh is better, but not by as much as you probably imagine. Most Americans today have never tasted what vegetables used to taste like before industrial farming took over. Such produce still exists in some parts of the world, but it is becoming hard to find even in Russia.

The problem with fruits and vegetables that lack flavor is that our brain doesn't recognize that we have eaten enough. Our senses are not satisfied until our gut is so bloated that it physically can't hold any more. That becomes the "shut off" signal that our brain responds to, rather than the psychological satisfaction of having acquired enough nutrition, as determined by taste.

Compounding this, human beings become conditioned during childhood to recognize what constitutes a "meal". If children grow up getting high-protein and high-fat meals, that's what every meal will seem to require. This is one of the principle differences in how Americans eat compared to most of the rest of the world. Put these two factors together and you have the reason for national obesity. The recipes here are to reduce meat intake in a comfortable way. You won't come away from these dishes feeling like you had a salad for dinner. However, there is a fair amount of work in making most of these compared to just frying up some chicken, of course.

Ultimately, remember that we are trying to do something that's technically impossible—turning vegetables into meat. Some of the simulations here are extremely good, but rather than judging every dish as a comparison to meat, I suggest that you just taste each dish without preconceptions. That attitude will go a long way in making an enjoyable dietary transition to lower meat consumption.

Salmagundi and Farrago

These are two terms you will encounter here that you've probablly never heard before. Within the context of this book, a _salmagundi_ is a mixture with hard boiled egg that you can eat with bread as a small meal. It is packed with flavor and nutrition.

A _farrago_ is something that is intended as an ingredient in a more complex dish. It is a working material. Although you could eat it directly, it is a bit like eating peanut butter from a jar with a spoon.

NOT ALL PROTEIN IS CREATED EQUAL

There is a myth widely believed by vegetarians that it doesn't matter where your dietary protein comes from. This is simply not true. Proteins are made of chains of amino acids, but the relative proportion and digestibility vary a lot between plant protein and animal protein. Some of the amino acids that we must consume in order to be healthy are much lower in vegetable protein sources. Furthermore, the protein in vegetables is less easily absorbed. It is a fact that our digestive system works at optimum efficiency with animal proteins. This is especially the case for the sulfur-containing amino acids, which play a vital role in our health and are much more abundant in animal protein than from plants.

HOWEVER, there is no question that most western people eat far more animal protein than is healthy—but eating absolutely no meat has negative health consequences, too. My advice is to find a balance that you are comfortable with and not to completely eliminate meat from your diet. Moderation is the key.

If you can't stand the thought of animals being killed, then you should know just how many are killed in the process of farming vegetables. Pesticides, the destruction of animal habitats and irrigation systems that dry up and destroy wildlife areas—and the shooting and trapping of animals that eat crops, are all part of commercial farming. I lived on a small organic farm for a few years. During that time numerous deer were killed along with raccoons, chipmunks, groundhogs and birds. Not to mention rats, mice and thousands of insects, in case you're a Buddhist.

Organic farming doesn't mean letting animals eat your crops. Animals are treated as pests and dealt with accordingly. When you look at the produce aisle in a grocery store, you don't see the animals that were killed, but really you might as well be looking at the meat counter. Sorry to break it to you, but strict vegetarianism for the sake of saving animals is an illusion, unless the only animals you care about are cows, pigs and chickens.

WHAT KIND OF VEGETARIAN ARE YOU?

Ovo-Lacto Vegetarianism includes eggs and dairy products such as milk, and cheese. <u>The recipes in this book are all in accord with this.</u> Although many Ovo-Lacto Vegetarians also eat fish and fish products such as salmon, Worcestershire sauce and caviar, <u>no</u> fish or fish product is required in any of the recipes in this book.

Lacto Vegetarianism includes dairy products but not eggs.

Ovo Vegetarianism includes eggs but not dairy products.

Buddhist Vegetarianism. Different Buddhist traditions have different teachings on diet, and they are generally more strict for monks and nuns. Many interpret the teaching of *not to kill* as not to consume meat, but not all Buddhists follow this. This has became controversial in recent years among many Buddhists for the reasons explained on the previous page.

Su Vegetarianism excludes not only all animal products but also vegetables in the allium family. Namely, onions, garlic, scallions, leeks, chives and shallots.

Fruitarianism permits only fruit, nuts, seeds, and other plant matter that can be gathered without harming the plant.

Jain Vegetarianism includes dairy but excludes eggs and honey, as well as root vegetables. That is, no potatoes, carrots, beets, onions, garlic, radishes, etc.

Sattvic Diet (also known as yogic diet), a plant based diet which may also include dairy and honey, but not eggs. It also excludes anything from the onion or leek family, red lentils, durian fruit, mushrooms, blue cheese, any fermented foods or sauces, all alcoholic drinks as well as coffee, black or green tea, chocolate, nutmeg and permits only small amounts of other spices.

Veganism excludes all animal flesh and by-products, such as milk, honey, and eggs, as well as items refined or manufactured through any such product, such as bone-char refined white sugar or animal-tested baking soda.

Raw Veganism includes only fresh and uncooked fruit, nuts, seeds, and vegetables. Vegetables can only be cooked up to about the boiling point of water. A dehydrator is allowed.

BEANS & LEGUMES

Thanks to the Internet where anyone can write anything, the disitinction between beans and legumes is now very confusing due to a tremendous amount of misinformation. The fact is that all beans are legumes. So are peas and lentils. The tastes vary, but from a nutritional point of view we can put them all in the same general broad category.

Name	Calories per 100 grams	Protein per 100 grams	Common Available Forms
Black Beans (also known as Turtle Beans)	130	8.2 grams	Canned and dried.
Chickpeas (also known as Garbanzo Beans)	164	8.9 grams	Canned and dried.
Cranberry Beans	136	9.3 grams	Dried. Also canned in some countries.
Fava Beans (also known as Broad Beans)	110	7.6 grams	Fresh, frozen, canned and dried.
Great Northern Beans (white beans are similar)	118	8.3 grams	Canned and dried.
Green Beans (also known as Haricot Vert)	28	1.5 grams	Fresh, frozen and canned.
Kidney Beans	127	8.7 grams	Canned and dried.
Lentils	116	9 grams	Dried.
Lima Beans	115	7.8 grams	Canned and dried.
Peas (green)	53	3.2 grams	Fresh, frozen, canned and dried.
Pinto Beans	143	9 grams	Canned and dried.
Soybeans	173	16.6 grams	Frozen (edemame) and dried.

All of the figures are for 100 grams (3.5 oz) cooked by boiling and without salt.

PSEUDOCEREALS

Pseudocereals are non-grasses that are used in the same way as cereals. Their seed can be ground into flour. Examples include amaranth, quinoa and buckwheat. Below are some comparisons.

As in the previous table, the figures are for 100 grams (3.5 oz) cooked by boiling without salt.

PROPERTY	WHITE RICE	BROWN RICE	LENTILS	BULGUR WHEAT	QUINOA
CALORIES	130	112	116	83	120
FIBER	0.4 g	1.8 g	7.9 g	4.5 g	2.8 g
FAT	0.3 g	0.8 g	0.4 g	0.2 g	1.9 g
PROTEIN	2.7 g	2.3 g	9.0 g	3.1 g	4.4 g
CALCIUM	10 mg	10 mg	19 mg	10 mg	17 mg
IRON	1.2 mg	0.5 mg	3.3 mg	1.0 mg	1.5 mg
MAGNESIUM	12 mg	44 mg	36 mg	32 mg	64 mg
ZINC	1.2 mg	0.6 mg	1.3 mg	0.6 mg	1.1 mg
COPPER	0.1 mcg	0.1 mcg	0.3 mcg	0.1 mcg	0.2 mcg
MANGANESE	0.5 mg	1.1 mg	0.5 mg	0.6 mg	0.6 mg
SELENIUM	7.5 mcg	9.8 mcg	2.8 mcg	0.6 mcg	2.8 mcg
VITAMIN B_6	0.1 mg	0.1 mg	0.2 mg	0.1 mg	0.1 mg
FOLATE	58 mcg	4 mcg	181 mcg	18 mcg	42 mcg
*GLUTAMIC ACID	524 mg	472 mg	1400 mg	973 mg	580 mg

*Glutamic acid is the naturally occurring MSG in foods after being digested. The only difference between glutamic acid and the MSG used as a seasoning is that the latter is sensed by your tongue.

MEDICINAL INGREDIENTS

One of the problems with a diet that is mostly fruits and vegetables is that it can cause intestinal gas and sometimes bad breath. Here is a reference guide to preventative measures you can use.

INGREDIENT	COMBATS	NOTES
Parsley	Bad breath, especially from garlic.	Fresh and uncooked works best.
Asafoetida	Intestinal gas	Very strong taste, but you only need a little.
Ginger	Indigestion	Fresh, pickled and dried are all effective.
Apple Cider Vinegar	Indigestion	Use in place of white vinegar when possible.
Fennel and Caraway	Intestinal gas	Whole raw seeds are the most effective.
Cloves	Bad breath, especially from indigestion	Unfortunately, low efficacy (it takes a lot)
Peppermint	Bad breath	Easier to use in a dessert after a meal.
Bulgur Wheat	Cardiovascular disease	One of the only foods proven to actually reduce the risk of heart attacks.

Ideally you will include one or more of these in cooked dishes, but which one you can use will vary with the dish because the flavor should never be compromised.

SUBSTANCE ABUSE

By this I mean the "abuse" of the substances themselves—to either transform them or utilize them as a natural flavor, rather than directly consuming them as food. The definition of a natural flavor was well defined in the 2012 United States Code of Federal Regulations (Title 21, Part 101) as follows:

"The term natural flavor or natural flavoring means the essential oil, oleoresin, essence or extractive, protein hydrolysate, distillate, or any product of roasting, heating or enzymolysis, which contains the flavoring constituents derived from a spice, fruit or fruit juice, vegetable or vegetable juice, edible yeast, herb, bark, bud, root, leaf or similar plant material, meat, seafood, poultry, eggs, dairy products, or fermentation products thereof, whose significant function in food is flavoring rather than nutritional."

SMOKED VEGETABLES

Potatoes

Think of potatoes as a blank canvas, since they have little flavor on their own. They provide a means by which to introduce a smoky flavor with either a soft or crisp mouth feel, depending on the cooking method employed.

Eggplant

By smoking eggplant that has been seasoned and previously cooked, you can imitate salami and other smoked meat products.

Chili Peppers

This is a well established technique in Mexico and South America. Chipotle chilies are smoked jalapeño chilies. The word chipotle comes from the Aztec word, *chilpotle*, which means "smoked chili pepper" (of any type). You can use a stove top smoker to transform any chili pepper in this way, as well as bell peppers.

CARAMELIZATION

Corn

There is enough sugar in corn that it can be caramelized some, especially if catalyzed with baking soda. The resulting product has notes that are pleasantly fish-like. The texture is rough, so it usually needs to be puréed and strained.

Carrots

With their high sugar content, carrots are especially prone to changing their properties upon prolonged heating. The key is that most of the water must be driven off first in order for the temperature to rise enough to allow caramelization to occur. This can't be done quickly, or you will skip right past caramelization to pyrolysis (see below).

PYROLYSIS

This is the process of cooking something to the point where it is actually starting to burn. Of course it must be stopped short of total combustion. This is a powerful technique to alter both flavor and mouthfeel, but it is only useful in a few instances. Any fruit or vegetable that has a significant amount of sugar or protein will become bitter and often acrid. However, there are some notable exceptions, particularly among the nightshade family.

Eggplant

This is one of the best vegetables for blackening slightly. Doing so creates rich, deep flavors that can be leached out into sauces.

Peppers

This is commonly used to blister the skin so that it can be removed, leaving behind a sweeter and more concentrated flesh.

Tomatoes

Like peppers, tomatoes can also be blistered to facilitate removing the skin, leaving behind sweeter and less watery pulp. However the deeply caramelized skin of tomatoes is rich in polyphenol compounds that can help simulate meat. The stringy and chewy texture is usually objectionable though, so the charred tomatoes are puréed and passed through a sieve to retain the flavor but exclude the tough membranes.

Corn

Dry roasting corn under a broiler until it just starts to burn does bring out some meat-like flavors but the texture is quite awful, being a mix of very chewy and sticky with occasional rock hard bits. Never the less, this can be utilized if it is blended with a liquid and then passed through a food mill. It's not very efficient, because most of the corn will be left behind on the sieve, but there are flavors that can't be achieved in any other natural way.

Napa Cabbage

Roasting the leaves up to the edge of pyrolysis produces a slightly bitter dry herb-like substance that is a beautiful counterpoint to sweetness, as illustrated in *Vegetarian Dynamite* (page 38).

Onions

Blackening onions on a dry pan is a well established cooking method in many parts of the world. European cuisine is actually an exception for not employing this. Possibly because the blackened onion flavor is best paired with hot chili peppers, which are not part of haute cuisine.

ENZYMATIC REACTIONS

Enzymes are easily denatured and rendered inactive, so all of the applications using them must be carried out with uncooked materials and generally not much above room temperature.

Peroxidase

Fresh butternut squash is well known for causing severe skin irritation. The cause is often wrongly attributed to an allergic reaction. The actual cause is a type of enzyme called a *peroxidase*. This is also found in horseradish, and to a lesser extent in broccoli.

Cysteine Proteases

These are a class of enzyme found in kiwi fruit, papaya, pineapple and figs. Each one is slightly different. In all cases the enzyme in the unripe fruit is more active. Kiwi is the most active of all. Unripe kiwi is commonly used in Korean cooking as a meat tenderizer. The enzyme is so powerful that the surface of the meat will turn into nasty slime if left for too long.

Cysteine proteases also react with other non-meat proteins, such as those in soy, mushrooms, beans, etc. The purpose then is not to tenderize, but to alter the structure, and indirectly, the flavor.

Alliin Lyase

Also known as *allinase*, this is the enzyme in garlic that produces the pungent aroma and taste. A small amount of fresh garlic has a profound effect on onions, leeks, chives and all members of the Brassica family (cabbage, cauliflower, broccoli, Brussels sprouts, etc.) This was explained in great detail in Volume 3 of the *Cooking in Russia* series.

Blue Cheese

This is rich with enzymes, but unfortunately the type sold in stores is usually pasteurized and processed to the point where the enzymatic activity is dead. If you can get unpasteurized blue cheese, then you have something to experiment with. None of the recipes here rely on this, because relatively few people will be able to get fresh unpasteurized blue cheese.

FERMENTATION

Some of the recipes in this book call for beer, wine and spirits. These are all the result of fermentation and the subsequent aging in wood barrels which produce a mind-boggling array of flavor molecules. The alcohol is nearly all evaporated during cooking, but the flavor molecules are less volatile and thus, left behind.

All fermentation adds complex subtle flavors. Aside from spirits, this applies to vinegar (especially balsamic vinegar), cheeses, bread (especially sourdough), sauerkraut, soy sauce, miso, kimchi and more.

Some flavors can be produced by home fermentation of fruits and vegetables with yeast, or even bacteria. However, there are many potential hazards involved with this, not the least of which is that it is illegal for individuals to do at home in the United States and other nations. However, it is a method used commercially and one of the ways that flavorings are manufactured, just so you know.

OTHER TRICKS OF THE TRADE

When it comes to imitating meat flavors, the king of all seasonings is MSG (monosodium glutamate). Mushrooms, tomatoes and cheeses are all very high in natural MSG, so these are all key ingredients you will see used many times here.

Nuts are another common substitute for meat among vegetarians, particularly Buddhists. Just a little bit can add a great deal of texture and richness.

Thyme is intimately associated with roast chicken in the subconscious of most people. Using a good deal of thyme (especially fresh thyme) will usually bring chicken to mind. In the same way sage brings turkey to mind for most people, particularly Americans because sage is the dominant flavor of traditional Thanksgiving turkey and stuffing.

Among all of the seasonings routinely used in cooking, the most valuable spice for meaty deceit is cumin, which when combined with other flavors can supply the backbone of meat flavor. You'll find cumin is used extensively here. Stock up.

Coffee is another ingredient that we don't usually think of as tasting like meat, but in small amounts it is a powerful source of tannins and other flavor molecules found in roasted meats.

Tea can be a great secret ingredient for flavor resonance. See *Cooking in Russia, Volume 2* (page 25). Tea is a symphony of thousands of flavor molecules, especially polyphenols. The complexity and importance of these in the *psychology of flavor perception* was explained in some detail in Volume 3. Some teas are blended with flavorings that are not sold directly to consumers, such as the bergamot in Earl Gray Tea. These are a rich source of flavonols, which are essential in the manipulation of flavors. The selection and method of combining these to achieve a particular result is as much of an art as it is a science. The recipes in this book were the result of a great deal of experimentation, but the key is that certain non-meat ingredients either have elements that are meat-like that can be exploited, or they can be cooked to transform them into something more meat-like.

BALSAMIC VINEGAR

Balsamic vinegar is a perfect example of an ingredient we don't think of as being meat-like, but it contains flavors that are in the same category. However, inexpensive supermarket brands are often nothing more than ordinary vinegar with caramel coloring and artificial flavoring. Such products are completely worthless for delivering the complex aromatic flavors and polyphenols that are developed during the slow barrel aging by traditional methods.

Even stepping up a bit to the next tier of balsamic vinegars, these are generally produced on an industrial scale in vats and not aged at all. These may be fine for some applications, but they will not bring the background flavor notes to the dish that are the magic of real balsamic vinegar.

What is referred to as *TBV* (Traditional Balsamic Vinegar) is extremely expensive and sold only in 100ml (3.5 oz) bottles. After extensive searching and testing, I recommend the product shown below for all of the recipes here that call for Balsamic vinegar.

Giuseppe Giasta of Modena is the original maker of Balsamic Vinegar in the world. Their products are ranked from 1 to 5 gold medals. The 2 gold medal, *Il Classico* (250ml), is ideal because it is aged in oak and has had centuries old balsamic mixed in with it to enhance the flavor. The price is still affordable, especially since you will only use a small amount at a time. This is the best value you can find in an authentic product.

BROISE COOKING METHOD

Broise (pronounced *broo-wahz*) cooking is a hybrid between broiling, roasting and braising. Food to be cooked is spread out on a shallow metal cooking tray. This is covered either with foil, or with a layer of parchment and then foil over that (if the ingredients are acidic). In both cases, the foil is crimped down snugly around the edges. Then this pan is placed 15cm (6 inches) from the broiler element of a hot oven with fan assist on.

View inside of an oven looking up at the broiler element.

This method is especially useful in creating deep flavors in vegetables without burning. The temperature is generally kept between 150° and 180°C (300° to 355°F). Cooking times can range between about 30 minutes to over an hour. The infrared radiation of the broiler penetrates the foil, gently caramelizing the top layer. The small volume of air and the sealed-in moisture creates a braise, and the metal pan becomes hot from the circulating air, which roasts the bottom of the mixture by conduction at the same time.

Some of the recipes in this book will work with an easy-to-find small aluminum cake pan, but not for those containing tomatoes or

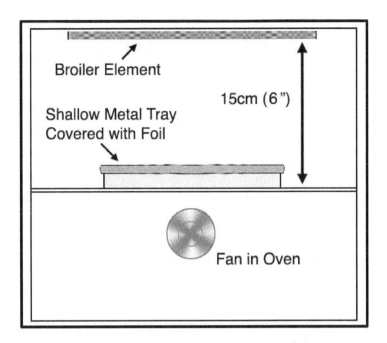

Broiler Element

15cm (6")

Shallow Metal Tray
Covered with Foil

Fan in Oven

anything acidic. Stainless steel is the way to go, and such a pan will last forever—even in heavy restaurant use they last for decades. You'll want to get the right equipment for the best results. What you need is a commercial restaurant *stainless steel insert pan* (that's what it will be called in a restaurant supply shop) that's a 1/6th size (restaurant pans are measured by the fraction they are of a "full sheet", which is larger than home consumer ovens). You want a shallow one. It is easy to find one that's 6.5cm (2.5 inches) high, but ideally you want it to be even more shallow, which is what I'm using, but that's not a standard size and very hard to find.

If you buy one of these from a restaurant supply shop it will be inexpensive (less than you paid for this book). While you are there, you might want to get a larger 1/3 size pan (but just as shallow) in case you will scale up some of these recipes in the future. Such pans are sometimes sold in gourmet cooking stores in shopping malls, but you'll pay much more there. Most restaurant suppliers will sell to the general public, and there is always online shopping.

DEGUSTATION DINING

Some of the finest (and most expensive) restaurants in recent years serve meals as a series of tiny courses—sometimes as many as 30 courses over a period of 3 to 4 hours. There are often only two choices for the diner: Meat/Fish or Vegetarian. A diner who selected the vegetarian option would be angry paying hundreds of dollars for a series of small plates of different steamed vegetables and sliced fruits, of course. So restaurants must come up with ways to produce interesting dishes that are made from fruits and vegetables, but pack enough flavor and body that a miniscule degustation-size portion will not seem like a leaf of lettuce on a plate for an astronomical price.

Some of the recipes presented here are best suited to being this sort of small courses as part of a large degustation menu, because that's exactly the purpose that I created them for. I realize that this is difficult to arrange in an ordinary household, where meals are generally based around a single entrée. An item like the *Beet Loaf* (page 88) is far more enjoyable as a very small portion between other vegetarian dishes than it is as an entrée. Restaurants have an enormous advantage in this regard, because of the high volume and the number of cooks available. You will probably discover that some of the recipes here are better suited to when you have a large dinner party or event, and you need a dozen or more small plates. Some recipes make good side dishes and appetizers, too.

Drinking eight glasses of water in a day is extremely difficult for most people, yet drinking eight glasses of wine during the coarse of a degustation dinner can happen almost by accident!

WATER CONTENT

The relative water content of vegetables vs. proteins is behind why meat lovers can't be satisfied with vegetarian cuisine.

FOOD	WATER	PROTEIN
Beef	50 %	28 %
Veal	70 %	19 %
Chicken	68 %	27 %
Pork	72 %	25 %
Fish	70 %	21 %
Eggs	90 %	10 %
Broccoli	91 %	2.8 %
Carrots	87 %	0.9 %
Mushrooms	89 %	3.1 %

As you would expect, vegetables are mostly water and have far less protein. By reducing water through cooking, the relative percentage or protein increases. For example, if we cook broccoli so that the water has been reduced from 91% down to 50% (that of beef), the protein content increases from 2.8 to 5 percent. Except that purging water from vegetables is fairly easy, so we can actually reduce the water in broccoli down to about 15% through careful cooking, which effectively increases the protein content to 17% - that's approaching the protein content of veal or fish.

In addition, when the protein content increases to such a high relative percentage, the Maillard Reaction is now facilitated, since with less water the temperature it cooks at can be higher and the Maillard Reaction requires about 150°C (300°F) to proceed.

Vegetarian Recipes

...FOR CARNIVORES! All of the recipes here have stronger flavors and more substance to them than what we usually think of as vegetarian fare. Anyone can make a salad and call it a vegetarian meal, but you'll be hungry again very soon after eating it. The vegetarian recipes here will fill you up as much as any meat-centric entrée. Obviously this does not mean they are low-calorie or fat-free or low-carb, or cholesterol-free or any other popular dietary trend. You can't have everything. If you want a lot of flavor out of vegetables that will be hearty and satisfying, there is no magical way to produce that without calories, including fat and carbs.

I would become a vegetarian if there was such a thing as a bacon tree.

(see next page)

FAKON POTATO SKINS

Fakon (rhymes with bacon), as in fake bacon. You will swear there is bacon in these, but there's none at all—or any other meat. Just multiply all of the ingredients to scale it up

4 pieces	Smoked Potato, halves (page 124)
45g (1.5 oz)	Zucchini, diced very small
45g (1.5 oz)	Cheddar Cheese, grated
15g (0.5 oz)	Scallions, chopped
2 teaspoons	Flour
1/2 teaspoon	Mediterranean Meat Spice (page 142)
1 teaspoon	Smoked Paprika (Pimentón)
2 T	Olive Oil (in all)
	Sour Cream for serving (optional)

ADDITIONAL INFORMATION

When making the smoked potato halves, use the same method as described on page 124. but cut the potatoes so they can be used as skins.

The first step of this recipe involves making a preparation that you may find has wider applications. If you taste the Zucchini Nuggets you will immediately recognize the remarkable meat-like properties. When they are broiled, they also acquire some of the mouthfeel of roasted meat.

PROCEDURE

1. Combine the diced zucchini with 1/2 teaspoon of the smoked paprika in a bowl. Toss to combine well.

2. Add the flour and toss to combine again.

3. Add 1 tablespoon of the olive oil and mix well.

4. Heat a nonstick skillet on a medium-high setting (#7 to 8 out of 10). When the pan is hot, add the zucchini mixture and stir frequently until it is

quite brown (but not burnt). This will take about 5 minutes.

5. Transfer the contents of the pan back to the bowl and toss with the Mediterranean Meat Spice while it is still warm. Now you have the Zucchini Nuggets described in the above paragraph on the previous page.

6. Scoop out the centers of the four smoked potatoes, taking care not to go too deep and break the skins up.

7. Put the potato pulp into the bowl of a food processor along with the cheddar cheese and scallions. Pulse a few times until the contents look a bit like they were diced 0.5cm (0.2 inch cubes). This happens in just a few pulses. Don't turn it into a purée.

8. Transfer the contents of the food processor to a bowl and gently mix with <u>half</u> of the fried zucchini by hand.

9. Use this mixture to fill the potato skins. Each one will be mounded up some, but the amount should be just about perfect for filling them.

10. Divide out the rest of the fried zucchini to top each potato with.

11. Sprinkle with the other 1/2 teaspoon of smoked paprika, dividing evenly.

12. Pour the other tablespoon of olive oil into the bottom of a metal baking tray. Spread the oil around and then place the stuffed potatoes down on the oiled surface.

13. Preheat oven broiler to 160°C (320°F) and position the shelf 15cm (6 inches) from the heat source.

14. Broil for approximately 20 minutes, however broiers vary quite a lot so you will have to keep a watch on it. Don't remove it unless you see that it is actually burning. It needs to cook very well to complete the simulation of the bacon.

15. Allow to cool for about 10 minutes. Serve with sour cream and a smattering of additional chopped scallions, if desired.

ASPARAGUS IN BUTTERNUT SQUASH AND BLUE CHEESE CREPES

Crepes that incorporate butternut squash, blue cheese, or even both are well established fare. Wrapping asparagus in crepes is also a classic, but between the richness of the sauce and the blue cheese, what would be a light brunch item becomes a satisfying course.

400g (14.1 oz)	Asparagus, fresh
360ml (12.7 oz)	Milk
150g (5.3 oz)	Butternut Squash
30g (1 oz)	Blue Cheese (strong or mild, as you like)
140g (4.9 oz)	Flour
2 whole	Eggs
3/4 teaspoon	Salt
150g (5.3 oz)	Aurora Sauce (page 132)
	Butter or Vegetable Oil

PROCEDURE

1. Trim the raw butternut squash of the skin and seeds so that you have just the pulp of the plant you are weighing. Chop this coarsely and put in a food processor with the blue cheese. Grind to coarse meal.

2. Transfer the contents of the food processor to a bowl. Cover with cling film. Leave it to stand out at room temperature for 2 hours. After that it is best if you refrigerator the mixture for 2-3 days, but that isn't absolutely necessary. The flavor and texture will improve, though - there are active enzymes in both the blue cheese and the butternut squash that are slowly reacting (see page 22).

3. Break the asparagus off at the weakest point along the stem to ensure

that the rest will be tender. Square off the ends and trim any coarse fibers.

4. Bring a skillet of salted water to a rapid simmer and cook the asparagus until just tender. The time will depend on the diameter of the asparagus.

5. Chill in an ice bath, then transfer to a storage container and reserve in the refrigerator until needed.

6. Put the butternut squash and blue cheese mixture into a blender along with the flour, salt, eggs and milk. Blend to purée.

7. Leave the batter stand at room temperature for 30 minutes before proceeding.

8. Heat a 23cm (9 inch) nonstick skillet on a medium-high heat (#7 out of 10). Add butter or vegetable oil to the pan as it heats.

9. Ladle out about 65ml (2.3 oz) of the batter into the skillet, swirling to coat evenly. Fry until a golden brown pattern has formed on the down-facing side. This will take 3-4 minutes.

10. Flip and cook the other side for about 2 minutes.

11. Transfer to a plate and cover with a sheet of paper towel to keep the next one from sticking to it.

12. Repeat the process from step #9, adding more butter or oil as necessary, until you have used all of the batter.

13. Preheat the broiler to 170°C (340°F). Adjust the oven shelf to be about 13cm (5 inches) from the heat source.

14. Coat the bottom of an ovenproof casserole dish with a little vegetable oil to keep from sticking. Place a crepe down, then some of the previously cooked asparagus. Fold the crepe and top with Aurora Sauce. Line up several crepes in this manner.

15. Broil until the sauce is just starting to brown. The exact time will depend on your broiler. When it is about a minute from being ready, you can add a sprinkle of the Louisiana Crumble from Volume 3 of Cooking in Russia, and return it to the broiler for the last 45 seconds or so.

VEGETARIAN SCHNITZEL

Although not totally convincing as veal, never the less it's surprisingly hearty and satisfying as vegetarian dishes go. This is also a fun example of how flavor chemistry works as two seemingly incompatible ingredients (broccoli and orange liqueur) combine and produce a completely different flavor.

250g (8.8 oz)	Blackwood Rice (page 121)
120g (4.2 oz)	Broccoli, previously frozen is okay
50g (1.75 oz)	Soy Meat Substitute (page 98)
28g (1 oz)	Hazelnuts
22g (0.75 oz)	Shallots or Red Onion
1/8 teaspoon	Cayenne
1 teaspoon	Olive Oil
1 1/2 teaspoons	Grand Marnier (see note below)
2 whole	Eggs
about 2 T	Butter, or substitute vegetable oil
	Mushroom Gravy (page 130)
	Parsley, fresh

GRAND MARNIER

This is an essential part of the flavor chemistry of this dish. This orange liqueur completely hides the notes of baked broccoli. It's almost like a flavor eraser, as you will see when you add this ingredient. You can substitute Cointreau with acceptable results, but Grand Marnier is better.

PROCEDURE

1. Grind the hazelnuts in a food processor until there are no large pieces remaining.

2. Whether you are using frozen or fresh broccoli (fresh is better), boil it in lightly salted water until just tender.

3. Drain the broccoli and add to a food processer bowl along with the

Blackwood Rice, Soy Meat Substitute, shallots. Grind until it is a homogeneous coarse meal. Scrape down the sides a couple of times to help with this.

4. Coat the bottom of a shallow metal baking tray with the olive oil (see Broise cooking (page 26). Cover the tray with foil, crimping down the edges tightly. Preheat oven to 160°C (320°F).

5. Switch the oven to broil with fan assist ON, and put the tray in on a shelf 15cm (6 inches) from the heating element. Cook for 30 minutes.

6. Remove the tray from the oven and allow to cool for 5-10 minutes before lifting the foil off.

7. Scrape the contents out to a bowl and leave to cool for another 10 minutes or so.

8. Stir in the Grand Marnier while it is still warm (but not too hot).

9. When the mixture is close to room temperature, mix in the eggs.

10. Heat a nonstick skillet on a medium heat (#6 out of 10). Put about a tablespoon of butter in the pan and wait until it foams up.

11. Working in two batches, add the mixture into the hot batter and shape like cutlets as it is cooking. Turn them over a couple of times during the frying for a total of 6-7 minutes cooking time.

12. Warm the Mushroom Gravy if it was prepared earlier. Either pour the gravy over the top of each cutlet, or serve it on the side as you prefer. Garnish with freshly minced parsley. You may also consider mustard and lemon on the side.

> *Tip: Cook corn on the cob in a pressure cooker with butter added to the water. Keep the pressure just at the point that steam is venting for about 45 minutes.*

VEGETARIAN DYNAMITE

Dynamite is a Japanese version of a French dish that's made with scallops. The sauce in the Japanese restaurant version includes masago. This sauce is more complex, which helps make up for the replacement of the seafood with zucchini.

375g (13.2 oz)	Mushrooms (in all)
250g (8.8 oz)	Zucchini
50g (1.7 oz)	Kiwi fruit
3 slices	Onion
1 T	Vodka Chili Elixir (see note below)
2-3	Kaffir Lime Leaves, dried (optional)
1/2 teaspoon	Mediterranean Meat Spice (page 142)
2 T	Chinese Dragon Cabbage (page 125)
100g (3.5 oz)	Mayonnaise
	Vegetable Oil
	Lemon Juice, fresh

ADDITIONAL INFORMATION

You can replace the Vodka Chili Elixir with Sriracha and still have good results. You can also use both if you like it really spicy.

The Kaffir lime leaves are a nice touch, but if you can't get them don't be afraid to make the recipe anyway. It will still be very good.

PROCEDURE

1. Peel the kiwi fruit. The weight specified is without the skin.

2. Combine the kiwi fruit with 100 grams (3.5 oz) of the mushrooms and 50ml (1.7 oz) of water with a stick blender (or if you are scaling this up, with a regular blender). Purée. Ideally, let this resulting paste stand for 30 minutes before proceeding to improve the final texture.

3. Preheat oven to 170°C (340°F). Scrape the mixture into a bowl.

4. Cut the zucchini into 1.5cm cubes (0.6 inches). Stir the zucchini cubes in with the puréed mushroom and kiwi mixture. Spoon this into a shallow metal baking tray as explained for the Broise cooking method (page 26).

5. Place the rings of onion on top of the mixture. Place a kaffir lime leaf on top of each slice of onion (if you have them). Cover tightly with foil.

6. When the oven is at temperature switch the heat source to broil and place the tray on a shelf positioned 15cm (6 inches) from the broiler element. Cook for 40 minutes.

7. During this time, cut the rest of the mushrooms into halves or quarters, as necessary to approximately the same size that you cut the zucchini cubes. Brown the mushrooms in a nonstick skillet on top of the stove using a little vegetable oil. Sprinkle lightly with salt when they are browned and transfer to a bowl.

8. When the time is up, remove the tray from the oven and rest at room temperature for another 10 minutes without removing the foil.

9. Discard the onion pieces and the kaffir lime leaves. Transfer the rest of the contents to the bowl with the mushrooms. Also add the Mediterranean Meat Spice, the Vodka Chili Elixir and 1 tablespoon of the Chinese Dragon Cabbage. Stir to combine and then let the mixture rest for a few minutes. You can refrigerate it at this point for up to a day without any adverse effects.

10. Stir in the mayonnaise. Spoon into ramekins or au gratin dishes. Place under the broiler 12.5cm (5 inches) from the heating element for about 8 minutes, but your time may vary so watch it. You want it to just start to be browning, but with no black char.

11. Remove from the broiler. Squeeze a little fresh lemon juice over each portion. Now sprinkle on the rest of the Chinese Dragon Cabbage, dividing it evenly. A sprinkle of Japanese Togarashi Pepper is a nice addition if you have it.

ARROGANT SOBA

This was one of my original menu items for Magenta Fusion back in 2001. It was wildly popular. Unfortunately the restaurant went under instantly when the property owner decided to increase the rent by 850%. We received requests for the recipe for this almost every day. This is the first time the recipe has ever been revealed.

350ml (12.3 oz)	Arrogant Bastard Ale (see note below)
150g (5.3 oz)	Soba Noodles, ideally SenSoy brand
1 T	Olive Oil, extra-virgin
1 teaspoon	Salt
	Vodka Chili Hot Sauce (page 139)
	Tomatoes, vine ripened heirloom
	Parmigiano-Reggiano, freshly grated
	Carrot Comestible (optional; page 119)
	Thyme, fresh
	Black Pepper, freshly ground

ARROGANT BASTARD ALE

This is from an American brewery, and where the dish got it's name from. Outside of the United States this is difficult to find. An excellent substitute is Trio *Extra Stout* from United Dutch Breweries, which is sold in most of the world. Failing that, choose a very stout ale with a good deal of bitterness.

PROCEDURE

1. Combine the ale with 175ml (6.2 oz) water in a sauce pan and bring to a slow boil.

2. Add the soba noodles. After they soften enough to wilt and slide down into the ale, add the salt. Maintain at a simmer until nearly all of the ale

and water have been absorbed.

3. Transfer the noodles to a bowl. There should be almost no liquid left behind. Add the olive oil to the noodles and toss to combine. These can be used right away, or refrigerated in a closed container for up to 2 days. When you need them, you can either microwave a portion for a few seconds, or if you are in a restaurant, put them in the steam convection oven. When warm, season to taste with the Vodka Chili Hot Sauce.

4. Put a portion of the noodles on a plate. If they are cold, then warm them as described in Step #3. Put a little of the Carrot Comestible down in the center of the noodles (if you are using it).

5. Add a little freshly grated Parmigiano-Reggiano over the top (to taste - but not too much).

6. Scatter diced fresh tomatoes around the edge of the plate, then a little ground black pepper. Finally add a few freshly picked thyme leaves.

IS PARMIGIANO-REGGIANO VEGETARIAN?

There are some extremist vegetarians who complain that imported Parmigiano-Reggiano is not an approved food because of the animal rennet used to make it. In the United States most cheese manufacturers now use synthetic rennet for separating the whey from the curds, but in Italy traditional methods are mandatory. Natural rennet is produced from the lining of a cow's stomach, however no cows are killed specifically for that reason. It is a byproduct of the meat industry and only about 1/4 of a teaspoon (about half a gram) of the substance is used per 4 liters (1 gallon) in making the cheese. If you still object to this, then you can substitute Parmesan made elsewhere with synthetic rennet, but the flavor will suffer.

SAMBAL CAULIFLOWER

In spite of the considerable spiciness of this quasi Malaysian dish (for those not accustomed to such heat), this is so delicious that you will probably eat the entire recipe by yourself before anyone else gets a chance to taste it. I'm not kidding!

285g (10 oz)	Cauliflower
45ml (1.5 oz)	Peanut Oil
45ml (1.5 oz)	Lime Juice, freshly squeezed (in all)
40g (1.4 oz)	Red Serrano Chilies (in all)
25g (0.9 oz)	Shallots, peeled
12g (0.4 oz)	Ginger, peeled and sliced thinly
1-2 cloves	Garlic, diced
2 teaspoons	Brown Sugar, ideally Muscovado
1/2 teaspoon	Turmeric
1/2 teaspoon	Salt
1/4 teaspoon	Black Pepper, ground
1/2 teaspoon	MSG
3 1/2 T	Cilantro, freshly chopped
3 T	Red Onion, sliced in thin strips
2-3 T	Vodka Chili Elixir (page 138)
1 whole	Star Anise
5cm (2 inch)	Cinnamon Stick
1 T	Chinese Dragon Cabbage (page 125)

RED CHILIES

You can substitute other types of chilies if you can't get red serranos chilies. Hatch (also known as New Mexico chilies) are a good replacement. Don't use chilies that have too much heat or character, such as Habañero or Jalapeño chilies, or the balance will be completely off. To make this milder, you can leave off the other 20 grams (0.7 oz of the sliced chilies that are added to the sauce. To make it even milder yet, scrape the membranes and seeds out of the half that go into the stick blender.

PROCEDURE

1. Put half of the red chilies, half of the lime juice, the shallots, ginger, garlic, brown sugar, turmeric, salt, black pepper, 2 tablespoons of the cilantro and all of the peanut oil into the cup of a stick blender and purée until there are no large lumps left.

2. Cut the cauliflower into slices about 6cm (1/4 inch) thick. A lot of it will crumble, but that's okay. Set it aside for now.

3. Slice the other half of the red chilies into rings.

4. Heat a large nonstick skillet on medium-high (#7 out of 10). When it gets hot (about 100°C or 210°F), add the puréed mixture from the stick blender along with the sliced red chilies, the star anise pod and the cinnamon stick. Stir and wait for it to begin to sizzle.

5. Now lower the heat slightly (#6 out of 10) and fry the mixture for 2-3 minutes, stirring occasionally.

6. Add the cauliflower to the pan. Stir to coat the pieces evenly with the mixture. Cook for about 3 minutes with frequent stirring.

7. Add 30ml (1 ounce) water to the pan and put a lid on. Lower the heat to medium (#5 out of 10) and cook for 7 minutes without stirring it.

8. Remove the lid and continue cooking for another 1-2 minutes until the cauliflower is the right tenderness to eat—but not mushy.

9. Now add the rest of the lime juice, the Chinese Dragon Cabbage and another tablespoon of cilantro. Cook for one minute with stirring.

10. Turn the heat off. Remove the star anise and the cinnamon stick. Sprinkle the MSG on and stir for another 30-45 seconds.

11. Transfer to a plate. Sprinkle with the Vodka Chili Elixir. Add the sliced red onion strips over the top and finally the last half tablespoon of cilantro. Serve with white rice.

TOFU FAJITAS

Most of the fajitas served in American Mexican restaurants are very mild compared to the authentic dish. This version has more of a kick than you might be used to, but that also helps make the tofu to seamlessly replace the meat.

180g (6.3 oz)	Tofu, extra-firm (see note below)
45ml (1.5 oz)	Orange Juice, preferably fresh
15ml (0.5 oz)	Lime Juice, fresh
15g (0.5 oz)	Chipotle Chilies in Adobo (canned)
15g (0.5 oz)	Garlic cloves, peeled and chopped
1 1/2 teaspoons	Cumin Seeds
1 teaspoon	Coarse Salt
3/4 teaspoon	Jalapeño Chili Powder (see below)
1/2 teaspoon	Oregano, dried
1/2 teaspoon	Cilantro, dried
1/2 teaspoon	Black Peppercorns
30g (1 oz)	Corn Flour (fine cornmeal)

Corn Oil and additional Lime Juice
Also Red and Green Bell Pepper and Onion

PREPARING THE TOFU

Cut the tofu into cubes about 2cm (3/4 inch) on all sides. Then put the pieces between sheets of paper towel and press to expel moisture. Change the paper towel a couple of times to get as much of the liquid out as you can. The weight called for is after the tofu has been dried in this manner.

JALAPEÑO CHILI POWDER

Dried and powdered jalapeño chilies are ideal for this, but may be difficult to find depending on what country you are in. You can substitute other ground dried chilies.

PROCEDURE

1. Put the cumin seeds, coarse salt, oregano, cilantro and black peppercorns in an electric spice mill and grind to a powder.

2. Into the cup of a stick blender, combine the orange juice, lime juice, chipotle chilies in adobo, garlic cloves and ground spices from the previous step. Purée.

3. Put the prepared tofu into a bowl and add 30 grams (1 oz) of the mixture from Step 2. Mix to combine, taking care not to break up the tofu.

4. Add the corn flour to the same bowl and gently toss to coat evenly.

5. Put a large nonstick skillet on a medium-high heat (#7 out of 10). When it is hot, add enough corn oil to cover most of the bottom. Wait for the oil to get hot, then add the coated pieces of tofu. Cook for 4-5 minutes until there it is golden brown on the bottom (life up pieces to check).

6. Now turn each of the pieces over and cook another 4-5 minutes until it is golden on the other side.

7. Drain on paper towels. Wipe out pan carefully with a wad of paper towel and add a little more fresh corn oil to the pan along with some onions and bell pepper cut into large strips. Cook without stirring very much until it is very well cooked (on its way to burning) before adding the rest of the fajita sauce from Step 2. Let it sizzle and stir the vegetables for a couple of minutes.

8. Add the cooked tofu pieces back to the pan and toss to combine. Cook for another couple of minutes, then transfer to a plate.

9. Season with lime juice liberally. Taste and add salt and a little MSG (bottles containing a mixture mostly of salt and MSG are commonly sold to Mexican restaurants under the name "Fajitas Seasoning", in case you think Chinese restaurants are the only places using this routinely).

10. A little fresh cilantro is a typical garnish.

FAUX TROUT ALMONDINE

This dish is actually a version of Sole Meuniere, another French classic. The traditional accompaniment is green beans.

2 pieces	Faux Fried Fish Fillets (page 106)
50g (1.75 oz)	Butter
30g (1 oz)	Almonds
2 T	Parsley, freshly minced flat leaf
2 cloves	Garlic
1/2 teaspoon	Pink Peppercorns, crushed
25ml (0.9 oz)	Lemon Juice, fresh
Additional parsley and lemon for plating	

THE ALMONDS

Blanched and slivered almonds are ideal, but you can also used whole almonds that you chop up with a food processor (though not as elegant).

PROCEDURE

1. Set a nonstick skillet on a medium-high heat (#7 out of 10). While it is getting hot, crush the garlic cloves against the side of a chef's knife and grind the pink peppercorns in a mortar.

2. Add the butter, garlic and crushed pink peppercorns to the pan. Stir as the butter melts and foams up. Some prefer more butter than this, too.

3. When the butter is quite hot, add the fillets to the pan. Brown lightly.

4. Turn the fillets over and add the almonds and the parsley to the pan.

5. When the fillets are lightly browned on the other side, turn them back over and reduce the heat. Add the lemon juice and cook another minute.

6. Sprinkle with salt. Remove the garlic cloves. Transfer to a plate and pour the pan sauce over. Add a little more parsley and wedges of lemon.

VEGETARIAN REUBEN SANDWICH

This is one of my personal favorite vegetarian recipes of all time. Normally a Reuben sandwich is made with sauerkraut and corned beef, but if you close your eyes it is nearly impossible to tell that there's no corned beef in this. Plus, it even looks quite a bit like chopped corned beef in both color and texture.

125g (4.4 oz)	Red Cabbage, chopped fine
70g (2.5 oz)	Pomegranate Farrago (page 114)
22g (0.75 oz)	Butter
15g (0.5 oz)	Parmesan Cheese, grated
1/2 teaspoon	Coarse Salt

Bread, Swiss Cheese, Mustard, Thousand Island Dressing

PROCEDURE

1. Heat a large nonstick skillet on medium-high (#7 out of 10). Add the butter to the pan. When it foams up, add the cabbage and the coarse salt. Sauté 3 minutes.

2. Add the Pomegranate Farrago and stir to combine well. Reduce heat to medium (#5 out of 10) and cover. Cook for 3 minutes.

3. Remove the lid to stir, then return the lid and cook another 3 minutes.

4. Remove the lid and stir in the parmesan. Cook another 2-3 minutes.

5. Season with fresh ground black pepper to taste. Set aside.

6. Grill bread, or put butter on one side of each piece and fry on a griddle or nonstick pan. Rye bread is traditional, but sourdough is excellent here.

7. Assemble two sandwiches with the Farrago mixture plus Swiss cheese, mustard and thousand island dressing. If you don't have thousand island, you can combine mayonnaise, ketchup and minced pickles.

BROILED GLOBE SQUASH SALAD

This is a remarkably delicious salad to prepare when tomatoes are at their peak of ripeness and available freshly picked. This is lighter than most of the recipes in this book, but still satisfying and hearty compared to typical vegetarian dishes.

Globe Squash
Cheese, grated (see note below)
Onion, minced
Tomatoes, vine ripe - best quality heirloom
Basil, fresh
Cilantro, fresh
Chives, fresh
Lemon Juice
Walnuts (optional - see note below)
Scallions
Vegetable Oil

ADDITIONAL INFORMATION

There are no fixed proportions to this dish. It will depend on your personal preference and sensibility.

Jack cheese is a safe choice if you are making this for guests or in a restaurant. Parmesan is a very good addition. If you are going to add walnuts, toast them first. Good quality halves are much better than small pieces here.

PROCEDURE

1. Make a conical cut at the top to remove the stump of the vine. Repeat this on the opposite side to remove the tough end there, as well. Now slice the globe squash into "steaks" about 2.5cm (1 inch) thick. Then run a knife around the edge to remove the outer skin.

2. Lay the squash slices down on a metal baking tray. Coat the top lightly with vegetable oil. Sprinkle with salt.

3. Position a shelf in the oven 15cm (6 inches) from the broiler element. Preheat oven to 170°C (340°F) and roast the squash for about 20 minutes with fan assist ON. It should be lightly browned on top. If not, give it longer.

4. Remove the squash from the oven and sprinkle with the cheese and then a little minced onion. Return under the broiler for a few minutes to melt the cheese. Watch it closely to keep it from burning.

5. During steps 3 and 4 above, prepare the salad topping as follows. In a bowl combine tomatoes cut into large diced pieces, freshly torn basil leaves, minced cilantro, a few snipped chives and a squeeze of lemon juice. Toss to combine, then put the bowl in the refrigerator until it is needed.

6. When the squash comes out from the broiler, allow it to cool for 3-4 minutes before transferring it to plates. Then top with the tomato salad, mounding it up in the center. Add the walnuts last, if you are using them. Finally add a tiny wisp of scallion on top.

Globe Squash

THAI STYLE FAUX FISH CURRY

This is a spicy dish, as it should be. The heat helps to conceal the imitation fish. You can make this with real fish, too.

2 pieces	Faux Fried Fish Fillets (page 106)
200g (7 oz)	Coconut Milk, unsweetened
150g (5.3 oz)	Shallots or substitute onion
1 whole	Green Serrano Chili, fresh
1-3 whole	Thai Chilies, dried (or substitute fresh)
1 stalk	Lemongrass
20g (0.7 g)	Ginger, thinly sliced
18g (0.6 g)	Garlic, peeled and chopped
2 1/4 teaspoons	Curry Powder (see note below)
1 T	Dark Brown Sugar, ideally Muscovado
1 T	Rice Wine Vinegar
1 T	Lime Juice, fresh
15g (0.5 oz)	Cilantro - stems and leaves separated
1 teaspoon	Coarse Salt
Vegetable Oil	

CURRY POWDER

Ideally use the Edwardian Fish Curry Powder recipe from *Cooking in Russia*, Volume 2 (page 197), or MDH brand curry powder from India.

PROCEDURE

1. MAKE THE SAUCE: Peel and slice the shallots into rings.

2. Trim the lemongrass and bash it a few times with the back of a large knife to bring out the fragrance.

3. Heat a small stock pot or large sauce pan on medium (#6 out of 10). When it is hot, add 30ml (1 ounce) vegetable oil.

4. When the oil is hot, add the shallots. Stir to break up the rings for a couple of minutes.

5. When the shallots have softened, add the lemongrass. Lower the heat slightly (#5 out of 10). Stir occasionally as the onion gradually becomes golden. If it is cooking too fast, turn the heat down further.

6. After about 5 minutes, add the sliced ginger. Continue stirring occasionally for about 9 more minutes.

7. During this time, dice the fresh green chili. Put it in a mortar with the dried chilies, garlic, cilantro stems and salt. Grind to combine well. Alternatively you can use a small food processor for this, but a mortar and pestle is the traditional way.

8. Now add the rice wine vinegar and lime juice to the mortar and grind some more.

9. The onion should be golden by now. Remove the lemongrass now. It may have broken up into several pieces, so be sure you get all of them.

10. Add the curry powder and stir well for about 20 seconds.

11. Add the mixture from the mortar, scraping the bottom to dissolve any fond from the onion in the liquid. Turn on your ventilation!

12. Add the coconut milk. Bring to a simmer and cook 5-6 minutes.

13. Pour the contents into a blender. Add the dark brown sugar and purée well to ensure there are no stringy bits of ginger in the sauce. This can now be bottled and stored in the refrigerator for up to two days.

14. MAKE THE FISH: Heat a nonstick skillet on medium-high (#7 out of 10). When it starts to get hot, add a little vegetable oil.

15. When the oil is hot, add the faux fish fillets (rare-side down) and cook until lightly brown.

16. Lower the heat (#4 out of 10). Add the coconut curry sauce from the first part. Bring to a slow simmer. **Optional: You can also add pieces of the Faux Seafood (see page 104) at this point.**

17. Transfer to a plate. Coarsely chop the cilantro leaves and add on top. You can also add thinly sliced red chilies for color. Serve with rice and wedges of lime on the side.

✦

CAULIFLOWER CAVIAR

The word "caviar" has two meanings in Russia. One is fish roe, as everyone knows. The other is a kind of cold appetizer dip that was originally made from cooked eggplant, tomatoes and onions. In more recent times the term has been applied to a variety of vegetable dishes that are served as a cold (or room temperature) appetizer with bread for dipping or spreading.

420ml (14.8 oz)	Vegetable Broth (page 119)
280g (10 oz)	Cauliflower, fresh
180g (6.3 oz)	Tomato Purée (passata)
120g (4.2 oz)	Bulgur Wheat, dry (uncooked)
100g (3.5 oz)	Apricots, dried
35ml (1.2 oz)	Olive Oil
28g (1 oz)	Shallots, minced
2 teaspoons	Deep Undertones Spice (page 142)
1 whole	Chili Pepper, fresh

Onion, Mayonnaise, additional Olive Oil (see text below)

PROCEDURE

1. Chop the cauliflower coarsely and the apricots into small pieces. Remove the stem from the chili, but leave it otherwise whole.

2. Put the vegetable stock, cauliflower, apricots, bulgur wheat, red chili and Deep Undertones Spice into a pressure cooker. Heat until it just comes to a simmer.

3. Put the lid on the pressure cooker and keep on a low heat (#2 out of 10) for about 40 minutes. Keep it below the point where steam is escaping. This is vital. The exact time will depend on the size of your pressure cooker and whether you have scaled this recipe up or not. When you open the pressure cooker, the liquid should have all been absorbed and the

mixture is just barely starting to stick to the bottom.

4. Open the pressure cooker and scrape out the contents to a bowl.

5. Heat a skillet on a high flame (#8 out of 10). When it is hot, add the olive oil and wait 30 seconds for the oil to get up to temperature.

6. Have a splatter guard ready in one hand when you add the tomato purée to the pan. Also add the whole red chili from the pressure cooker. Cover with the splatter guard.

7. Cook for about 3 minutes without stirring it.

8. Reduce heat slightly (#7 out of 10). Remove the chili. If you want it spicier, then dice the chili up and add it back in. Otherwise discard the chili. Add the mixture from the pressure cooker. Cook for 4-5 minutes with frequent stirring.

9. Reduce heat to medium (#5 out of 10). Add the minced shallots and cook for 1-2 minutes longer.

10. Taste and adjust with salt and black pepper. Add finely chopped onion and mayonnaise to taste. Plate portions with a ring mold, or just a scoop. Drizzle a little olive oil over the top and serve with warm rye bread.

✦

"How come they don't have mad-cauliflower disease?"

FRIED PEA CAKE SOUP

This delicious and hearty soup is reminiscent of Albondigas, only vegetarian and with exotic flavors from North Africa.

INGREDIENTS FOR PEA PATTIES

150g (5.3 oz)	Peas, frozen (see note below)
25g (0.9 oz)	Pea Flour (peasemeal)
25g (0.9 oz)	Flour
3/4 teaspoon	Turmeric
1/4 teaspoon	Salt
1 whole	Egg
1 T	Olive Oil

FOR SOUP

120g (4 oz)	Onion, cut in slices
120g (4 oz)	Potato, peeled and diced small
60g (2 oz)	Carrot, peeled and diced small
45g (1.5 oz)	Tomato Purée (passata)
30g (1 oz)	Garlic, peeled and chopped
30g (1 oz)	Goat Cheese (see note below)
15g (0.5 oz)	Cilantro, minced
1 T	Deep Undertones Spice (page 142)
1/4 teaspoon	Black Pepper, finely ground
Lime Juice, fresh	
Scallions	

ADDITIONAL INFORMATION

Boil frozen peas in salted water. When they are cooked, drain them and then weigh out the amount called for in the recipe.

A soft-textured mild goat cheese works especially well here, but you can substitute another mild flavored soft-textured cheese if you prefer.

PROCEDURE

1. MAKE THE PEA PATTIES: Boil the peas in salted water until tender (about 8 minutes).

2. Put the peas into the cup of a stick blender along with the pea flour, regular flour, turmeric, salt and egg. Purée. This will be difficult to purée.

3. Heat a nonstick skillet on medium-high (#7 out of 10). When it is hot, add the olive oil to the pan and wait 30 seconds.

4. Place small piles of about a tablespoon each of the pea mixture. Flatten gently. Fry in the oil until golden, then flip and cook the other side. Total cooking time should be 4-5 minutes per batch. Then set aside to cool.

5. MAKE THE SOUP: Heat a 3-4 liter stainless steel saucepan (do <u>not</u> use Teflon or cast iron for this) on high (#8 out of 10). When the pan is hot, put the sliced onions down on it with no oil. Don't move them around much. You want to cook them until they start to turn dark. The pan will be slightly scorched, but it will clean up later.

6. When the onions are turning dark, add the carrots and stir some. Reduce heat slightly (#7 out of 10). Cook another 4-5 minutes

7. Now add the potato and garlic. Cook another 2 minutes.

8. Add the tomato purée and Deep Undertones Spice Cook for another 2 minutes.

9. Add 1 liter (35 oz) water and the cilantro. Bring to a simmer. Adjust heat to maintain at a simmer. Cook for about 15 minutes.

10. Cut the pea patties into bite-sized pieces. Add the pieces to the soup along with the black pepper and continue simmering for 30 more minutes with a lid on. If you have a glass lid with a small hole in it, that's ideal.

11. The soup should be reduced in volume by now and be about the right consistency. If it is too thick, add water. If it is too thin, continue cooking it without a lid for a while longer. Taste and adjust the salt, but remember that the cheese will also add saltiness.

12. Ladle the soup out into bowls that can go under the broiler. Crumble goat cheese on top. Put a shelf about 12.5cm (5 inches) from the heating element and broil to make the cheese melt.

13. Add a little lime juice and some finely minced scallions to each bowl.

✦

FAUX LOBSTER THERMIDOR

Lobster Thermidor is my personal all time favorite dish, so you know that if I'm putting my name on an imitation, it's going to be worth your while.

120g (4.2 oz)	Faux Seafood (page 104)
70g (2.5 oz)	Mushrooms, regular champignons
60g (2 oz)	Butter (in all)
25ml (0.9 oz)	Cognac or Brandy
200ml (7 oz)	Milk (see note below)
30ml (1 oz)	Heavy Cream (33% fat)
2 T	Flour
45ml (1.5 oz)	Madeira, or Oloroso Sherry
1/2 whole	Onion, small
3 whole	Cloves (the spice)
1 whole	Bay Leaf, dried
2 teaspoons	Lemon Juice, fresh
3/4 teaspoon	Mustard, dry
3/4 teaspoon	Maggi Seasoning (optional)
22g (0.75 oz)	Parmesan Cheese, grated
2 slices	White Bread, ideally sourdough

THE MILK AND CREAM

Instead of the milk and cream, you can use 230ml (8.1 oz) of light cream, or half & half (as it is referred to in the United States).

PROCEDURE

1. Slice the mushrooms in halves, or quarters if they are large.

2. Heat a skillet on medium-high (#7 out of 10) and add 22 grams (0.8 ounce) of the butter to the pan. When it foams up, add the mushrooms. Fry until golden.

3. Flambée the mushrooms with the cognac (or brandy).

4. Put the mushrooms and any liquid from the pan in a bowl to cool. They will gradually exude more liquid which will be used in a later step.

5. In a small sauce pan, melt the remaining 30 grams (1 ounce) of butter over a medium heat (#5 out of 10).

6. When the butter has melted, add the flour and stir. Cook to form a blonde roux. See my video on roux if you are not sure how to do this.

7. During this time, stud the sliced side of the onion with the cloves.

8. Add the milk and the cream to the pan. Stir to combine.

9. Add the onion studded with the cloves (spice-side down), the bay leaf and the mustard. Cook slowly until thickened, stirring occasionally. This should take about 15 minutes.

10. Slice the Faux Seafood into large lobster-like chunks during this time. Also butter the bread lightly on both sides and cut into small cubes.

11. Now add the Madeira, the Maggi seasoning, and the juices that drained from the mushrooms to the pan. Stir to combine.

12. When the Béchamel is thickened, remove and discard the bay leaf and the pique (clove-studded onion). Pour into the bowl containing the mushrooms. Add the lemon juice and the pieces of Faux Seafood and stir gently to combine, taking care not to break up the pieces.

13. Divide into individual ramekins or *au gratin* dishes. Put the buttered bread cubes on top. Sprinkle with the grated Parmesan.

14. Cook under a broiler or salamander until the cheese is melted and the bread cubes are golden brown.

VEGETARIAN KOFTA

There are hundreds of different variations of Kofta, which are popular in Turkey, the Middle East and India. Kofta are usually made of ground meat, except in the case of Malai Kofta, which are made of curd. Kofta are especially popular in northern India served in a type of curry sauce like this. Mushrooms are not traditional, but there is virtually no mushroom taste in these.

300g (10.6 oz)	Faux Dark Chicken Meat (page 100)
200g (7 oz)	Onions, sliced into rings
160g (5.6 oz)	Tomato Purée (passata)
140g (4.9 oz)	Yogurt, plain (not low-fat)
75g (2.6 oz)	Gram Flour (ground dried chickpeas)
3 whole	Egg Yolks
30g (1 oz)	Ginger, peeled
30g (1 oz)	Garlic cloves (in all)
1 teaspoon	Cumin Seeds
3/4 teaspoon	Coarse Salt
1/2 teaspoon	Coriander Seeds
1/2 teaspoon	Dark Brown Sugar
5 whole	Cardamom Pods, green
5 whole	Cloves (the spice)
2 T	Coconut, dried (unsweetened)
15g (0.5 oz)	Cashews, ground
15ml (0.5 oz)	Peanut Oil
1 whole	Bay Leaf
1/8 teaspoon	Nigella
30ml (1 oz)	Cream, 22% fat
3-5 T	Lovecraft Coating (see note below)
about 3 T	Cilantro, fresh
about 2 T	Butter (or substitute more peanut oil)

LOVECRAFT COATING

The recipe is in Volume 3 of the *Cooking in Russia* series (page 242), You can substitute plain bread crumbs, but it will not be nearly as good.

PROCEDURE

1. Heat a stainless steel 2 to 4 liter pot on medium (#5 out of 10). When it is hot, add the peanut oil. When the oil is hot, add the onions. Cook for about 5 minutes with occasional stirring to break up the rings.

2. Add the bay leaf, cumin seeds, cardamom pods and coarse salt. Continue cooking with occasional stirring for 10 minutes.

3. During this time, chop 22 grams (3/4 ounce) of the garlic coarsely (the rest will be used later). Slice the ginger into julienne strips.

4. When the time has elapsed on the onions, add the garlic and ginger you just chopped along with the dried coconut, coriander seeds and cloves. Continue cooking with occasional stirring for about 3 more minutes.

5. Deglaze the pan with about 85ml (3 oz) of water. Scrape the bottom.

6. Add the tomato purée and nigella. Stir well. Reduce heat slightly (#4 out of 10) and partially cover with a lid. Cook for 20 minutes, stirring about three times during the cook time.

7. Turn the heat off. Add the yogurt, brown sugar and 150ml (5.3 oz) of water. Stir well and wait a few minutes for the mixture to cool down.

8. Transfer the contents to a blender. Purée, then pass through a sieve. Set aside for now as you make the kofta.

9. Crush the other 8 grams (0.3 oz) of garlic in a garlic press. Also mince a tablespoon of fresh cilantro. Combine the garlic and cilantro with the Faux Dark Chicken Meat and ground cashews in a bowl with the gram flour and egg yolks. Use the tines of a fork to mash everything together well. The resulting mixture should be a stiff chunky dough.

10. Divide the mixture into about 10 equal parts and form each into a small finger-size sausage shape. Roll each in the Lovecraft Coating.

11. Heat a nonstick skillet on medium (#6 out of 10) and add the butter. When it foams up, fry the kofta. Turn them around slowly and gently until they are golden brown on all sides.

12. Add the strained sauce to the pan. Reduce heat slightly. Simmer until it has been reduced by about half, then add the cream and stir. Garnish with fresh cilantro and serve with wedges of lemon.

GARLIC SOUP

This recipe uses the same enzymatic reaction explained in detail in Volume 3 of the Cooking in Russia series. This is a hearty and satisfying soup that's low in fat.

800ml (16 oz)	Vegetable Broth (page 119)
300g (10.6 oz)	Potatoes, peeled
100g (3.5 oz)	Cabbage, coarsely chopped
70g (2.5 oz)	Garlic cloves, peeled
1 1/2 teaspoons	Yucatan Spice Blend (see note below)
1 T	Butter

Cream (optional)
Parmesan, freshly grated
Parsley, fresh
Sherry Wine Vinegar (optional)
White Pepper, ideally freshly ground

ADDITIONAL INFORMATION

The procedure for making this seasoning is in Volume 3 of *Cooking in Russia* (page 223). As a substitute, put a whole bay leaf into an electric spice mill with half a teaspoon of coarse salt and grind to a powder. It won't have the same depth as the Yucatan Spice Blend, but it will work.

Although it is considerably more work, even better results will be obtained by replacing 100ml (3.5 oz) of the vegetable broth with the same amount of Espagnole from page 136.

PROCEDURE

1. Put the cabbage and 60 grams (2 oz) of the garlic into a food processor and grind it until there are no large pieces. Don't grind it too much because air has to be able to get to the pieces for the enzymatic reaction to take place.

2. Slice the potatoes on a mandoline set to 1.3mm (1/20th inch).

3. Put the butter on the bottom of a ceramic bread loaf pan. You don't need to melt it—you can just put little dots and it will melt later in the oven.

4. Put a single layer of potatoes down.

5. Sprinkle a little of the Yucatan Spice Blend on the potatoes.

6. Scatter some of the cabbage and garlic mixture from the food processor down on top of it.

7. Repeat steps 4, 5 and 6 until you have used up all of the potatoes and the cabbage mixture. Make sure you end up with a potato layer on top, but don't sprinkle the top with any of the ground spices. You may have noticed that up until now this is somewhat similar to the *Buddha's Blessing* recipe (page 86).

8. Cover with foil and roast at 160°C (320°F) for 3 hours with no fan.

9. Remove from the oven and scrape the mixture out to a blender. Add the rest of the garlic and the vegetable broth to the blender, too. Purée.

10. Pass through a sieve. At this point you can refrigerate it and keep it for several days, reheating any number of portions at a time.

11. Put the amount you wish to serve into a sauce pan. Add cream, if desired. Don't add cream to the soup before you store it in the refrigerator, or it will spoil much faster. Bring the soup up to a simmer on a medium heat (#5 out of 10) with occasional whisking. Maintain at a slow simmer for 5-6 minutes. Taste and adjust the seasoning with salt and ground white pepper.

12. Ladle into bowls and top with a little parmesan and fresh parsley. Try adding a little sherry wine vinegar, too. Because the vegetable stock is inherently sweeter than the chicken stock used in the non-vegetarian version, the sherry wine vinegar works even better here, adding a slight sweet and sour taste. Still, use it carefully or you'll have a vinegar soup.

REVERSE VEGETARIAN LASAGNA

This is the best no-pasta vegetarian lasagna that I've ever had, if I do say so myself. The "reverse" in the name is something you will only really understand after you taste it. What looks like the meat actually takes on the texture of the pasta in a traditional lasagna, and what would be the noodles takes on the role of the meat once you bite into it.

400g (14.1 oz)	Carrots, peeled
200g (7 oz)	Corn, canned
200g (7 oz)	Onion, peeled
60ml (2 oz)	Olive Oil (in all)
120g (4 oz)	Brown Rice (uncooked)
45ml (1.5 oz)	Lemon Juice, fresh
30g (1 oz)	Mayonnaise
1 1/2 teaspoons	Baking Soda (in all)
1 1/2 teaspoons	Hidden Salami Spice (page 141)
120g (4 oz)	Edam Cheese, sliced or grated
about 300g (10.6 oz)	Tomato Sugo (page 136)

ADDITIONAL INFORMATION

Try to get very large carrots. Note that you can do the first 8 steps of the procedure at the same time on the stove.

PROCEDURE

1. Boil the carrots in salted water until soft. Medium size carrots will take 16-18 minutes. Huge carrots will take longer. Then drain and cool.
2. Slice the onions into rings. Heat a medium skillet (stove setting #6 out of 10). When it is hot add a tablespoon of the olive oil, then the onions. Cook for 3-4 minutes.
3. Add half of the baking soda (1/2 tsp.) to the onions and stir. Continue cooking about 8 minutes until they are a goopy consistency. Set aside.

4. Rinse the canned corn in a sieve under running water. Drain well.

5. Heat another skillet (stove setting #6 out of 10). When it's hot, add the rest of the olive oil (about 45ml, or 1.5 oz). Add the corn to the pan. Cook for 3-4 minutes, then add the other 1/2 teaspoon of baking powder. Stir.

6. When the corn is browned well (about 10 minutes), transfer it to a bowl to cool. Pour about 20ml (1/3 oz) of the oil that the corn was cooked in into a clean sauce pan. Discard the rest of the oil.

7. Heat the saucepan on a medium-high setting (#7 out of 10). When the oil is hot, add the rice to it. Cook for about 5 minutes.

8. Add 230ml (8.1 oz) of water and the Hidden Salami Spice mixture to the rice. Bring to a boil, then reduce heat to medium (#4 out of 10). Put a lid on and cook until all the liquid is absorbed (about 45 minutes).

9. In the cup of a stick blender, combine the cooked corn and onions with about a third of the rice. Add the mayonnaise, lemon juice and 3/4 teaspoon of salt. Purée. Mix this back with the rest of the rice.

10. Use a mandoline to slice the carrots lengthwise about 1.2mm (1/20th inch) thick.

11. Put a little oil in the bottom of a shallow metal baking tray for use in the Broise method (page 26). Put down a single layer of the sliced carrots, overlapping edges slightly to cover the bottom completely.

12. Spoon half of the rice mixture down on top and smooth out. Then put another layer of carrots, then the rest of the rice mixture, then one more layer of carrots. Top with the Edam cheese. Cover with foil, but be sure that the foil is not in contact with the cheese.

13. Preheat oven to 160°C (320°F), then switch to the broiler for the heat source. Place the tray on a shelf 15cm (6") from the broiler element. Cook for 40 minutes.

14. Remove the foil and continue cooking until the cheese is bubbling.

15. Divide into portions and serve the pieces on top of small pools of the Tomato Sugo sauce. Add grated Parmesan, if desired.

CHICKLESS TCHOUPITOULAS

This classic dish of New Orleans lends itself to a vegetarian interpretation far better than you would ever imagine—until you taste it. The recipe is for 2 large portions or 4 small portions.

250g (8.8 oz)	Potatoes, waxy type
180g (6.3 oz)	Red Onion Farrago (page 112)
2 whole	Eggs
2 T	Corn Flour (fine cornmeal)
60-90g (2-3 oz)	Green Peppercorn Béarnaise (see below)
	Butter, Olive Oil
Optional:	Mushrooms
	Eggplant Salami (page 102)

PROCEDURE

1. Peel and dice the potatoes. Boil in lightly salted water until they are about half cooked. Don't cook them completely or they will turn into mashed potatoes by the end. The exact timing will depend on how large you cut the cubes and what specific type of potato you used, so you will have to judge for yourself. When they are done, drain them and set aside.

2. If you are going to use mushrooms, then either slice or quarter them (whichever you prefer) and fry them until golden brown in a mix of butter and olive oil. Then drain them, sprinkle with a little salt and set aside. Salting them earlier will inhibit browning as it draws out moisture.

3. Preheat oven to 175°C (350°F). Whisk the eggs in a bowl. Now fold in the Red Onion Farrago and corn flour.

4. Butter the bottom of a ceramic loaf pan, or some other ceramic or glass ovenproof dish that isn't too large. Spoon the egg mixture into the dish and roast for about 30 minutes until it is completely cooked. The exact time will vary some depending on the vessel you chose, so watch that it doesn't burn—and also that it's fully cooked when the time is up.

5. During this time, fry the potatoes in a nonstick pan on top of the stove in additional butter and olive oil. Also make the Béarnaise (see below).

6. When everything is ready, put some of the potatoes down on each plate. Then divide the mushrooms between the plates. Use a metal cake spatula to portion and lift rectangles from the oven-baked egg mixture onto each plate. Top with the Green Peppercorn Béarnaise. If you are using the Eggplant Salami, cut it into thin strips and put it on top of the Béarnaise. A little fresh tarragon is a nice addition if you have it.

GREEN PEPPERCORN BÉARNAISE

There is a video on the *Cooking in Russia* YouTube channel that shows how to make this. The recipe below is only slightly different for this dish.

22g (3/4 oz)	Shallots, minced
1/2 teaspoon	Green Peppercorns, dried
60ml (2 oz)	White Wine, a good oaky Chardonnay
30ml (1 oz)	Red Wine Vinegar
1 1/2 teaspoons	Tarragon, dried (in all)
90g (3oz)	Butter
2	Egg Yolks
1/2 - 2 teaspoons	Tabasco Sauce

PROCEDURE

1. Grind the green peppercorns in a mortar or with a spice mill.

2. Put the peppercorns into a saucepan with the shallots, white wine, red wine vinegar and half of the tarragon. Bring to a rapid simmer. Reduce until it is nearly dry, but not actually dry and burning. Watch it carefully.

3. Remove the pan from the heat and put in 60g (2 oz) of the butter. Let the residual heat melt it.

4. When it has stopped melting, add the egg yolks, the rest of the butter and the rest of the tarragon. Whisk together well.

5. Move the pan on and off the heat while whisking to finish cooking. Season with Tabasco to taste.

ZUCCHINI FILETS WITH GOAT CHEESE

The resonant triad of artichoke, yellow miso and goat cheese is the engine driving this bewitchingly addictive vegetarian dish.

about 4	Zucchini sections, 3cm (1.25 inch) long
92g (3.25 oz)	Artichoke Hearts, bottled (see below)
35g (1.25 oz)	Blackwood Rice (page 121)
25g (0.9 oz)	Carrot Comestible (page 119)
15g (0.5 oz)	Yellow Miso (Shinshu)
15ml (0.5 oz)	White Wine, dry
2 teaspoons	Lemon Juice, fresh
3/4 teaspoon	Hidden Salami Spice (page 141)
1 clove	Garlic
60g (2 oz)	Goat Cheese
2 T	Olive Oil, ideally Kalamata

ADDITIONAL NOTES

Select canned or bottled artichoke hearts that are <u>not</u> pickled. Those packed in oil are better, but drain the oil off before weighing.

PROCEDURE

1. Put the Blackwood Rice, artichoke hearts, Carrot Comestible, miso paste, white wine, lemon juice, Hidden Salami Spice and garlic into the cup of a stick blender and purée.

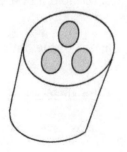

2. Use an apple corer to drive holes through the zucchini. These holes will often fuse together during cooking. Try to select the largest zucchini that you can find. Make four holes if the zucchini is very large (7.5cm or 3 inches) across. The cylindrical plugs you remove are not used in this recipe.

4. Use a spoon to fill the holes with the puréed mixture. Use the back of the spoon to press the filling down and smear a tiny bit across the top surface. The small amount on the top and bottom surfaces will caramelize and become part of the deep flavor.

5. Preheat the oven to 190°C (375°F). Pour the olive oil into the bottom of a ceramic or glass casserole dish that's large enough to hold all of the zucchini "steaks" in a single flat layer.

6. Put the pieces down into the oiled casserole dish, then turn each of them over so that the top surface is now lightly coated in the oil.

7. Put the casserole dish on a shelf in the center of the oven and set a timer for 20 minutes.

8. When the timer goes off, take the dish out and turn all of the zucchini pieces over. Return to the oven for another 20 minutes.

9. Remove the dish yet again and turn the pieces back over. Continue cooking for still another 20 minutes.

10. Turn the pieces over one last time. Turn the oven off, then put the dish back in the oven as it cools for 10 more minutes.

11. Remove the dish and turn the pieces over one last time. Cover with foil. Leave for at least 30 minutes at room temperature.

12. Cut the goat cheese into slices. Put a slice on each zucchini piece. You can use the same casserole dish they previously cooked in to finish. Turn the broiler on and position a shelf 15cm (6 inches) from the broiler element. Cook until the goat cheese has partly melted and browned at the edges. If the goat cheese just runs down the sides, then you didn't use a firm enough type.

13. You can serve these immediately, but really these are better if left to cool until just above room temperature. Add a few drops more lemon juice. Originally plated on a bed of spinach with Béchamel on the spinach and grilled prawns surrounding it.

ROASTED FENNEL WITH VALBRESO FETA

This makes a nice light meal atop angel hair pasta or spaghetti. Originally served with lobster butter on the pasta.

Fennel
Tomatoes
Blackwood Rice (page 121)
    or Faux Ground Beef (page 96)
Valbreso Feta, or other sheep milk type
Mozzarella
Mediterranean Meat Spice (page 142)
Olive Oil
Fresh Herbs (see recipe)

PROCEDURE

1. Trim the stems and coarse outer part from the fennel. Cut the bulb into slices measuring 6cm (1/4 inch) thick. Trim the tomatoes of the stems and cut them into 6cm (1/4 inch) slices, too.

2. Coat the bottom of a glass or ceramic baking dish with olive oil. Place the fennel slices down on that in a single layer.

3. Put about a tablespoon of Blackwood Rice down on each slice. Then add a tablespoon of the feta. Put a tomato slice on top of each one. Sprinkle lightly with the Mediterranean Meat Spice.

4. Cover with foil. Roast in a 200°C (390°F) oven for 40 minutes.

5. Remove foil and continue roasting another 30 minutes.

6. Remove from the oven and put a little mozzarella cheese on top of each one. Return to the oven for about 5 more minutes to melt the cheese.

7. Drizzle with a little olive oil. Add some finely minced herbs. Oregano and/or basil work especially well. Serve with buttered angel hair pasta or spaghetti.

ASIAN BRAISED BEETS WITH PEANUTS

Exotic far eastern flavors transform beets into a main course.

360g (12.7 oz)	Beets, peeled and cubed large
70g (2.5 oz)	Shallots, peeled and chopped
45g (1.5 oz)	Peanuts, shelled
35ml (1.25 oz)	Peanut Oil (in all)
20g (0.7 oz)	Galangal, peeled and chopped
10g (0.3 oz)	Ginger, peeled and chopped
22ml (0.75 oz)	Lime Juice, fresh
1 T	Brown Sugar, ideally Muscovado
1 teaspoon	Cumin Seeds
1/2 teaspoon	White Peppercorns
1/2 teaspoon	Coarse Salt
1 teaspoon	Deep Undertones Spice (page 142)

PROCEDURE

1. Grind the brown sugar with the cumin seeds, white peppercorns and coarse salt in an electric spice mill.

2. Into the cup of a stick blender, put 50ml (1.75 oz) water with the spices you just ground. Add the shallots, galangal and ginger (chop them up first or the blender won't be able to purée them). Also add the lime juice, 22ml (0.75 oz) of the peanut oil and the Deep Undertones Spice. Purée.

3. Put the beets into a braising dish that's just large enough to hold them in a single layer. Pour the mixture from the stick blender over them. Stir.

4. Braise in a 180°C (355°F) oven for 1 hour 45 minutes. During this time, fry the peanuts in the remaining peanut oil. Sprinkle with salt. Set them aside to cool for a while, then grind them up in a food processor.

5. When the beets are done braising, stir in the ground peanuts. Let the mixture cool for at least 30 minutes before serving. Season with crushed red chili flakes to taste.

INVISIBLE CHICKEN RICE

The chicken is what's invisible–not the rice. Sorry if I got your hopes up that this recipe would somehow defy the laws of physics. Although it is still a good magic trick, because almost everyone believes that this contains chicken. Scaling it up just means multiplying everything.

100g (3.5 oz)	Brown Rice
30ml (1 oz)	White Wine, dry
1 teaspoon	Mediterranean Meat Spice (page 142)
1 whole	Bay Leaf, Turkish - dried
1/4 teaspoon	Turmeric
1/4 teaspoon	Salt
200g (7 oz)	Aurora Sauce (page 132)
22g (0.75 oz)	Shallots, or substitute red onion
1 teaspoon	Olive Oil
2 branches	Thyme, fresh

PROCEDURE

1. Wash the rice under cold running water in a sieve.

2. Put the rice into a sauce pan along with 250ml (8.8 oz) water, the white wine, the Mediterranean Meat Spice, the bay leaf, turmeric and salt. Bring to a simmer on a medium heat (#6 out of 10).

3. Lower the heat slightly to maintain a slow simmer for 10 minutes with <u>no</u> cover.

4. Now cover with a tight lid and lower the heat further (#2 out of 10). Cook for another 20 minutes like this.

5. Turn the heat off, but leave the lid on for another 30 minutes or longer.

6. Open the lid and remove the bay leaf. Most of the liquid should have been absorbed. If it is very soupy, then heat without a lid until most of the liquid has evaporated or been absorbed. This will depend on the exact type

of rice you are using. The rice at this point should <u>not</u> be fully cooked.

7. Combine the rice with the Aurora Sauce in a bowl. Mix well.

8. Put the olive oil in the bottom of a metal baking dish, as described for the Broise cooking method (page 26). Coat the bottom evenly.

9. Spoon the mixture into the metal pan. Now sprinkle the minced shallots over it. Put the branches of thyme down on top on top of that. Seal the top over well with foil.

10. Preheat broiler to 160°C (320°F). Position shelf 15cm (6 inches) from the heat source. Roast for 30 minutes.

11. Now increase the oven temperature to 200°C (390°F). Leave the pan where it is in the oven and roast another 15 minutes.

12. Remove the pan from the oven to cool for 5-10 minutes before opening. Discard the thyme branches.

SIMPLE VARIATIONS

A healthy meal can be had by simply mixing some chopped fresh tomatoes and minced scallions with the Invisible Chicken Rice while it is still warm.

Take this in an Italian direction by sautéing sliced red bell pepper, tomatoes in olive oil. Add some crushed garlic during the last 30 seconds of cooking, and mix together with the Invisible Chicken Rice.

BIRIYANI-ISH MODIFICATION

Another option is to add 2 teaspoons of curry powder at the same time you mix the Aurora Sauce in (step #7). When it is cooked, top with some of the Cola Red Onions (page 120), or plain fried onions and fresh minced cilantro. This will produce a dish resembling Chicken Biryani. The Edwardian curry powder recipe on page 196 of Volume 2 is ideal for this.

FAUX PORK AND SPINACH PASTITSIO

Pastitsio is a classic Greek dish that is related to Lasagna, but made with layers of bucatini. Although beef, veal or lamb are the traditional fillings, more recently some people make this with pork and spinach, which is exactly what this tastes like, even though there is no actual meat in it.

300g (10.6 oz)	Maccheroncini or Bucatini pasta
350g (12.3 oz)	Béchamel Sauce (see note below)
180g (6.3 oz)	Green Farrago (page 110)
180g (6.3 oz)	Gouda Cheese, sliced or grated
120ml (4 oz)	White Wine, dry
2 whole	Eggs
60g (2 oz)	Red Onion, minced
45g (1.5 oz)	Hazelnuts
45g (1.5 oz)	Parmesan, grated
2 T	Parsley, freshly minced (or 1 tsp. dried)
2 teaspoons	Sherry Vinegar
1 1/4 teaspoons	MSG
1/2 teaspoon	Black Pepper, ground
1/4 teaspoon	Cinnamon, ground
	Olive Oil

ADDITIONAL INFORMATION

The amount of pasta will depend on whether you make it two layers or three. If three, then you need another 150 grams (5.3 oz) of the pasta and double the entire filling recipe. You will need 525 grams (18.5 ounces) of the Béchamel Sauce for three layers, but the same amount of cheese.

The preparation of Bechamel Sauce is a fundamental skill that all cooks should be familiar with. For 350 grams of the Bechamel, use 30 grams butter, 2 tablespoons of flour and 375ml of milk (preferably goat milk for this particular recipe). Simmer for 15 minutes to thicken.

PROCEDURE

1. Boil the pasta until it is al dente. Toss with a little olive oil and set aside to cool.

2. Prepare the Béchamel Sauce. Ideally, using goat milk.

3. Crush the hazelnuts in a mortar until they are coarse and crumbly.

4. Put the minced shallots in a sauce pan with the hazelnuts, white wine, sherry vinegar, parsley and black pepper. Bring to a boil, then reduce to a simmer and cook until it is reduced to a glaze.

5. Scrape the contents into the cup of a stick blender. Add the parmesan cheese, MSG and the eggs. Also add half of the Bechamel Sauce. Purée, being sure to blend the hazelnuts well, too.

6. Stir together (do not use the motorized stick blender) with the Green Farrago.

7. If you use a 32 x 24cm (12.5 x 9.5 inch) baking dish, you won't have to trim the pasta. If you choose a smaller dish, you will have the difficult task of cutting each piece of pasta to fit. Coat the bottom of the baking dish with a little olive oil. Lay the cooked tubes of pasta down in rows to form a solid base across the bottom.

8. Depending on how many layers you are going to make (a small dish could contain more, or you might be multiplying the recipe) divide out the mixture over the pasta. Then add another layer of pasta and either repeat with the rest of the filling and yet another layer of tubes, or continue.

9. Carefully spoon the rest of the Bechamel Sauce over the top layer of the pasta. Bake in a preheated 185°C (365°F) oven with NO fan assist for 45 minutes.

10. Remove the dish from the oven and put the cheese on top. Return it to the oven for another 10 minutes, or until the cheese is well melted.

11. Allow it to rest for at least 30 minutes before serving. This is especially good to make in advance and reheat the next day.

STUFFED BUNS

One great way to use the Farrago series (pages 108-116) is by baking them in small loaves of bread to create a sort of encapsulated sandwich. This method creates a soft bread.

325g (11.4 oz)	Flour (in all)
20g (0.7 oz)	Yeast, or 1 packet dry, but fresh is best!
1 teaspoon	Sugar, white
1/2 teaspoon	Salt (see note below)

PROCEDURE

1. Combine 25 grams (0.9 oz) of the flour with 120ml (4 oz) of water in a sauce pan. Bring to a simmer while scraping the bottom with a wooden paddle. Cook until it is thick, which should only take about 3 minutes.

2. Move the pan off the heat to cool. In the bowl of your stand mixer, dissolve the sugar in 150ml (5.3 oz) of warm water. Make sure it is *just* above body temperature. Now add the yeast and smear it into the solution. Wait 20 minutes for it to foam up. If it doesn't, then your yeast was dead.

3. Equip your stand mixer with the dough hook. Put the bowl in place and add 150 grams (5.3 oz) of the flour along with the salt and the previously cooked (gelatinized) flour solution from the sauce pan. Run the mixer slowly to form a *sponge*, then cover with a damp towel for 30 minutes.

4. Add the last 150 grams of flour. Knead with the dough hook for about 5 minutes. Then cover with a damp towel and let rise 45 minutes.

5. Put flour on your hands and pull a wad of dough off. Wrap the farrago of your choice inside, then place it on a silicone mat under a damp towel to rise for 2 hours more. Make similar buns with the rest of the dough.

6. Brush with eggwash, if desired. Bake at 200°C (390°F) for 18 minutes.

KOREAN STYLE VEGETARIAN GYOZAS

Simulates the kimchee and ground pork filling used.

140g (5 oz)	Chinese Cabbage
45g (1.5 oz)	Pomegranate Farrago (page 114)
28g (1 oz)	Carrot Comestible (page 119)
15g (0.5 oz)	Garlic, chopped
1 T	Vodka Chili Hot Sauce (page 139)
35ml (1.25 oz)	Sesame Oil (in all)
	Wonton Wrappers

PROCEDURE

1. Chop the cabbage up finely, selecting only the green leaves.

2. Heat a nonstick skillet on medium (#6 out of 10). When the pan is hot, add 28ml (1 oz) of the sesame oil. When that gets hot, add the cabbage and cook for about 4 minutes until it is soft and just starting to brown..

3. Add the garlic and continue cooking another 2 minutes.

4. Add the Pomegranate Farrago and Carrot Comestible. Stir. Reduce heat (#4 out of 10) and continue cooking until the mixture is golden brown (2-3 minutes more).

5. Transfer to the bowl to cool.

6. Stir in the Vodka Chili Hot Sauce and the rest of the sesame oil. Then refrigerate until cold (at least 2 hours).

6. Fill wonton wrappers with the filling using a gyoza press, or by hand if you are skilled enough. Originally chopped oyster was also included.

7. Fry in vegetable oil, or steam them if you prefer. You can also cook them in simmering water for a couple of minutes, drain them and then coat them with a little peanut oil and fry them later on demand for best results.

ROASTED ITALIAN CABBAGE

This is based on a traditional Italian recipe. Cabbage has long been a staple food among peasants, and many inventive ways of cooking it developed over time.

400g (14 oz)	Cabbage (no stem parts)
60g (2 oz)	Onion
60g (2 oz)	White Beans, canned (rinsed)
30ml (1 oz)	Olive Oil, extra-virgin
30g (1 oz)	Parmesan Cheese, grated
2 cloves	Garlic
2 whole	Bay Leaves
1 teaspoon	Coarse Salt
1 teaspoon	Austrian Spice Mix (see note below)
1-3 teaspoons	Vodka Chili Hot Sauce (page 139)
Bread Crumbs	
Eggplant Salami (optional - see below)	
Parsley, fresh	

ADDITIONAL INFORMATION

The full recipe for the Austrian Spice Mix is on page 221 of *Cooking in Russia, Volume 3*. You can substitute half a teaspoon each of ground caraway seeds and white pepper. Don't let the name *Austrian* fool you.

Fried pancetta or bacon was used in the original recipe, but you can either leave that out completely (it will still be quite good) or, better, you can substitute some pieces of the Eggplant Salami (page 102) at Step #5, as explained in the procedure below. The amount is up to you, but don't use as much as you would pancetta or bacon, or it will be overwhelming. The eggplant salami does not weigh very much by comparison, so 60 grams (2 ounces) would be far too much.

You can substitute chopped up Italian Diavoletto type red chilies in oil for the Vodka Chili Sauce if you want to keep it authentic to Puglia.

PROCEDURE

1. Coarsely chop the cabbage and onion. Put the pieces into a food processor and grind to small uniform pieces. Don't actually purée, though.

2. Heat a large nonstick skillet on a medium setting (#7 out of 10). When it is hot, add the olive oil. Wait about a minute for the oil to get hot, then add the cabbage and onions from the food processor bowl. Also add the bay leaves, coarse salt and spice mixture. Stir often to coat evenly with the oil. Cook about 5 minutes.

3. Lower the heat to medium-low (#4 out of 10) and put a lid on the pan. Cook for about 15 minutes.

4. During this time, mince the garlic with a knife and also chop about 2 tablespoons of parsley.

5. Remove the lid and stir to inspect the cabbage and onion mixture at the bottom. There should be some slight browning. If not, then replace the lid and cook longer. If it is actually burnt, then your pan was too thin, your heat was too high, or your lid was not secure. In that case you have to start over.

5. Increase the heat slightly (#6 out of 10). Now add the white beans, the parsley, the garlic and the chili sauce. This is also when you add the Eggplant Salami, if you are using it. Stir occasionally for about 5 minutes.

6. Now add the freshly grated parmesan cheese and turn the heat off. The residual heat of the mixture will melt the cheese in as you stir it.

7. At this point you can set the mixture aside for up to several hours, or refrigerate it for a few days, if you need to. When you are ready to continue, preheat your oven to 180°C (360°F). Either put the mixture into individual *au gratin* dishes, or into a single larger vessel for family-style service. Add bread crumbs over the top. Drizzle with olive oil, if desired.

8. Switch your oven to broil. Position shelf 10cm (4 inches) from the heat and cook for about 5 minutes until brown on top.

9. Add a little freshly minced parsely before serving.

CHINESE STIR FRIED PORKLESS RICE

Like most stir fried dishes, this is a culinary ballet that you have to rehearse to get perfect. The illusion of pork is very good, but don't try to make more than double the portion here at a time on a home stove because there isn't enough heat to cook it properly. Smaller portions like this will produce the best result if you don't have a proper restaurant type wok burner.

120g (4.3 oz)	Basmati Rice, cooked (see note below)
75g (2.6 oz)	Carrot Farrago (page 108)
60g (2 oz)	Onion
22g (0.75 oz)	Celery
15g (0.5 oz)	Ginger, grated
15g (0.5 oz)	Garlic, peeled
2 T	Peanut Oil (in all)
1 to 3 teaspoons	Vodka Chili Hot Sauce (see note below)
2 teaspoons	Soy Sauce
1 whole	Egg
3 T	Scallions, freshly chopped
1/2 teaspoon	MSG
1 teaspoon	Sesame Oil

ADDITIONAL NOTES

The recipe for the Vodka Chili Hot Sauce is in this book (page 139) - note this is the hot sauce with the vinegar added, and not the base Elixir. You can substitute Sriracha if you need to.

The rice should be dried out by having been made a day or two previously and stored in the refrigerator in a partially open container so that air can circulate. Other methods including leaving the rice in the pot overnight after you cooked it, or spreading out freshly cooked rice onto a metal baking sheet and roasting it at about 150°C (300°F) for 10 minutes or so. Then refrigerate it on a plate with no cover for 15-20 minutes.

PROCEDURE

1. Cut the onion into medium-size cubes. Chop the garlic into small pieces. Crack the egg into a bowl and whisk it well.

2. Heat a heavy-bottomed nonstick skillet or a wok on a high heat (#8 out of 10). When it is hot, add 1 tablespoon peanut oil. Wait until the oil is hot.

3. Add the onion to the pan. Sauté for about 2 minutes.

4. Add the celery and stir fry for another 1-2 minutes.

5. Add the ginger and garlic. Sauté for about 45 seconds, then push everything to the edges of the pan or wok.

6. Add the Carrot Farrago to the center of the pan. Stir fry the mixture in the middle of the pan for about 1 minute.

7. Push the Carrot Farrago toward the edges of the pan, forming an inner ring away from the onions, garlic and ginger at the edge. Add the other tablespoon of peanut oil in the center. Now add the rice to the center of the pan and stir fry for about 1 1/2 minutes.

8. Fold in everything from the edges of the pan. Stir fry for about 30 seconds to combine, then push everything back off to the sides, as before.

9. Pour the whisked egg into the center of the pan. Do <u>not</u> stir it. When it sets up firm (about 1 minute) add the soy sauce to the wet part of the egg. Wait until it is firm on the bottom, and then cut it up with the edge of the spoon you are stirring with. Don't blend it in - you want actual pieces. Turn down the heat to medium (#5 out of 10).

10. Add the Vodka Chili Hot Sauce (or Sriracha). Turn the heat off. Stir fry for another minute using the residual heat.

11. Add the MSG and the sesame oil. Taste to adjust salt level.

12. Add the freshly chopped scallions. Combine and serve. Offer soy sauce and additional Vodka Chili Hot Sauce or Sriracha on the side. Note that if you are not strictly vegetarian, a very small amount of actual roasted pork added at the end makes this dish seem loaded with meat.

SUPER TOSTADAS

This is a way to boost the flavor and satisfying sustenance of the lowly vegetarian tostado so that you won't miss the meat. The vodka is there to dissolve polyphenols, as explained in Volume 3. You will not taste the alcohol in the final dish because it evaporates during the frying of the tortillas.

COATING MIX	
30ml (1 oz)	Tequila
30ml (1 oz)	Vodka
30g (1 oz)	Chanterelle Mushrooms (see note below)
30g (1 oz)	Avocado, ripe
15g (0.5 oz)	Corn Flour, or substitute Oat Flour
1 teaspoon	Yucatan Spice Blend (see note below)
1/4 teaspoon	Salt

ADDITIONAL INFORMATION

You can substitute ordinary mushrooms, but the result will not be as good. Mushrooms are not native to Latin American cuisine, but it is chemically important here. Chanterelles contain polyphenols (specifically flavonols) as explained in Volume 3 of my cookbook series, that are only soluble in alcohol.

Note that corn flour is finely ground corn meal. Do not substitute corn starch, which is completely different. You can substitute oat flour with good results, but corn is best.

The procedure for making the Yucatan Spice Blend is on page 223 of *Cooking in Russia, Volume 3.* In this case if you don't have it, then substitute Chili Powder.

PROCEDURE

1. Put the tequila, chanterelles, avocado, corn flour, Yucatan Spice Blend and salt in the cup of a stick blender and purée.

2. Brush the mixture onto one side of each tortilla.

3. Heat a pan with the butter and the corn oil.

<u>PER EACH LARGE TOSTADO</u>

1 each	Large Flour Tortilla (22cm / 9 inch)
	if smaller, then scale accordingly
22g (0.8 oz)	Coating Mix (see above)
1 teaspoon	Butter
1 teaspoon	Corn Oil
3 T	Soy Meat Substitute (page 98)
30g (1 oz)	Tomato, vine ripened
30g (1 oz)	Avocado, cubed small
15g (0.5 oz)	White Onion, diced fine
1 1/2 T	Cilantro, minced
2 teaspoons	Lime Juice
1/4 teaspoon	Salt
2 T	Sour Cream or Creme Fraiche
Cheddar Cheese, grated (optional)	

4. Fry each tortilla, un-coated side down.

5. When it is well cooked on that side, flip over and lightly cook the other side.

6. Transfer to a plate. Now fry the Soy Meat Substitute in the same pan.

7. Put the cooked Soy Meat Substitute on each tostado and then add the rest of the toppings listed in the box above.

8. You can put the sour cream on top, or (as is traditional) serve it in a side dish. Also, this is traditionally served to accompany Pozole and certain other Mexican soups.

VEGETARIAN RAGU BOLOGNESE

This uses spices that are not traditional in Italian cooking, but the end result is a surprisingly good imitation of the classic.

150g (5.3 oz)	Tomato Purée (passata)
120g (4.2 oz)	Carrots
120g (4.2 oz)	Onions
120g (4.2 oz)	Tomatoes, fresh
80ml (2.8 oz)	Red Wine, dry (see note below)
45ml (1.5 oz)	Olive Oil (in all)
150ml (5.3 oz)	Milk, full fat (not skim milk)
30g (1 oz)	Shallots, minced
2-3 whole	Garlic cloves, peeled
1 teaspoon	Cumin seeds, whole
1 teaspoon	Coriander seeds, whole
1 teaspoon	Thyme, dried
1 whole	Star Anise
1 whole	Bay Leaf
3/4 teaspoon	Coarse Salt
3/4 teaspoon	Hidden Salami Spice (page 141)
2 sprigs	Basil, fresh (preferably Opal Basil)
45g (1.5 oz)	Faux Ground Beef (optional - see below)

ADDITIONAL INFORMATION

Bolognese is normally made with white wine, but some changes have to be made in lieu of the missing meat. You can bolster the meatiness further by adding a little *Faux Ground Beef* (page 96) at Step #3 and/or 45g (1.5 oz) of the *Demi Glace Replacement* (page 135) at Step #12.

PROCEDURE

1. Peel and trim the carrots. Boil in salted water for 16 minutes, then drain and cool to room temperature.

2. Coarsely chop the onions and fresh tomatoes. Combine in a food processor with the boiled carrots. Combine well, but do not purée.

3. Heat a large nonstick skillet on medium-high (#7 out of 10). When it is hot, add 1 tablespoon of the olive oil. Wait 30 seconds and then add the vegetables from the food processor along with the bay leaf. Stir occasionally and cook for 15 minutes.

4. During this time grind the cumin seeds, coriander seeds, star anise, thyme and salt in an electric spice mill. Also mince the garlic with a knife.

5. When the 15 minutes have elapsed on the vegetables, add the garlic and the spice mixture. Lower the heat (#6 out of 10) and stir for 2 minutes.

6. Transfer to a bowl to cool. Remove the bay leaf. You can store this for up to three days before continuing, if needed.

7. Heat a sauce pan on high (#8 out of 10). Add the rest of the olive oil to the pan when it is very hot and then wait about 30 seconds.

8. Add about a third of the tomato purée (passata) to the hot oil and quickly cover with a splatter guard. Wait 1 full minute. Do not stir.

9. Sprinkle the paprika and sugar onto the bubbling tomato purée. Wait another minute. Do not stir.

10. Scatter the chopped shallots across the top. Don't stir. Reduce heat slightly to #7 out of 10. Wait 3 minutes.

11. Add the previously cooked vegetable mixture. Stir. Cook 2 minutes.

12. Add the wine and the Hidden Salami spice. Stir. Cook 2 minutes.

13. Add the rest of the tomato purée and the milk. Stir occasionally while bringing to a simmer.

14. Lower the heat to medium (#4 out of 10). Add the spigs of fresh basil and cover. Simmer for 50-60 minutes. Lift the lid and stir it a couple of times during this period to make sure it isn't sticking at the bottom.

15. Remove the basil. Taste and adjust the salt. Remember that this will probably have Parmesan cheese served with it, which adds saltiness.

APPLICATIONS

Toss some with spaghetti or a flat-wide noodle. Plate, then add more of the ragu on top, and then grated Parmesan and minced parsley.

BRUSSELS SPROUTS SAMALGUNDI

Even children who think they hate Brussels sprouts nearly all love this for the rich, sweet and nutty flavors.

160g (5.6 oz)	Brussels Sprouts, previously frozen
100g (3.5 oz)	Potato, peeled
30g (1 oz)	Butter (or substitute olive oil)
15g (0.5 oz)	Garlic cloves
35g (1.2 oz)	Hoisin Sauce (see note below)
30g (1 oz)	Almonds
1 teaspoon	Coarse Salt
2-3 whole	Juniper Berries
3 whole	Bay Leaves
1 T	Red Wine, dry
2-3 whole	Sage leaves, fresh
1 whole	Hard Boiled Egg (optional)
2 T	Onion, finely minced

HOISIN SAUCE

This is a Chinese sauce made from a fermentation process you can't duplicate at home. Stokes, a company in the United Kingdom, makes a Hoisin sauce that's actually better than the Chinese variety for this recipe because it is not as strong and thick. I don't recommend Stokes' Hoisin for actual Chinese cooking, though. Lee Kum Kee is usually preferable.

PROCEDURE

1. Thaw the Brussels sprouts to room temperature. Do not boil them.
2. Combine the Brussels sprouts and the garlic in a food processor. Scrape down the sides as needed to obtain a uniform mixture - but not a purée. Most food processors are incapable of actually puréeing these ingredients, and will leave relatively large pieces, which is what you want. Let the mixture stand while you perform the next operations.

3. Toast the almonds on a dry skillet.

4. Cool the almonds at room temperature for a few minutes, then use a mortar and pestle or food processor to grind them with the juniper berries and coarse salt. Try not to have any large lumps at all.

5. Transfer to a bowl and stir together with the contents of the food processor and the Hoisin sauce.

6. Spread the mixture into a shallow metal dish. Slide the bay leaves down into the mixture, equidistant from each other. Cover with foil.

7. Place dish in an oven preheated to 180°C (355°F) using the Broise method (page 26). Roast for 50 minutes. Carefully peel back the foil to check for browning around the edges. If not, put the foil back and return it to the oven for a little longer..

8. Cool with the foil still on it for at least 30 minutes at room temperature.

9. During this time, cut the potato into small dice (about 5mm or 0.2 inch cubes).

10. Heat a nonstick skillet on medium (#5 out of 10). Add the butter to the pan and wait until it foams up. Now add the diced potato and stir to coat pieces with the butter evenly.

11. Reduce heat slightly (#4 out of 10). Cover and cook for 5 minutes.

12. Remove the lid and scrape the roasted Brussels sprouts mixture into the skillet, picking out the bay leaves (discard them). Stir to combine. Cook until almost dry (about 5 minutes).

13. Add the sage leaves to the pan and moisten with the red wine. Cook gently for about 8 minutes. Then cool the mixture and discard the sage.

14. Chop the hard boiled egg (if you are using it) and stir it in with the minced onion. Taste and adjust seasoning with salt, black pepper and a little MSG, if desired.

BUDDHA'S BLESSING

I took the name of this dish from a restaurant operated by actual Buddhist monks several decades ago. This is very similar to the most memorable item on their menu, and also one of the more alien types of dishes (though not unusual in terms of the way many monks eat).

500g (17.6 oz)	Potatoes, peeled
150g (5.3 oz)	Cabbage
22g (0.75 oz)	Garlic, peeled
2 T	Rice Flour
1 T	Peanut Oil, or vegetable oil
100g (3.5 oz)	Yogurt (not low fat)
1/4 teaspoon	Liquid Smoke

Pecans (see notes below)
Cola Red Onions (page 120)
Pickled Burdock (see below for more information)
Cilantro, fresh

ADDITIONAL INFORMATION

Use good quality pecan halves. The exact amount is up to you. Toast them lightly on a dry pan first. Don't use too many, either.

Pickled burdock is available in most Asian stores. It usually looks like very thin carrots, but tastes more of pepper. See alternative on next page.

PROCEDURE

1. Put the cabbage in a food processor with the garlic and process until homogenous. This is the enzymatic technique explained in Volume 3.

2. Preheat oven to 150°C (300°F) with <u>no</u> fan assist. Slice the potatoes on a mandolin to 1.3mm (0.05 inch).

3. Layer a ceramic bread loaf pan with potatoes, then a sprinkling of the cabbage and garlic mixture, then another single layer of potatoes, etc. Repeat until all of those ingredients are used.

4. Drizzle the oil over the top. Cover with foil and roast for 2 hours.

5. Remove the foil and continue roasting another 30 minutes.

6. Allow it to cool to room temperature.

7. Transfer to a bowl. Add the yogurt, rice flour and liquid smoke. Using the back of a fork, blend the ingredients well. Leave the potatoes in small sheets, though—don't mash it into a complete paste.

8. Preheat oven to 180°C (355°F) with fan assist ON, or 200°C (390°F) with no fan assist. Form several small piles or logs with the mixture on an ovenproof casserole dish or baking tray. Each mound will be a portion, so you can decide yourself how much that will be. Sprinkle each one lightly with sea salt.

9. Roast for 20 minutes. This was originally prepared in a wood burning oven, which is why a little liquid smoke has been added in this recipe. If you actually have a wood burning oven, then use that instead and omit the liquid smoke, of course.

10. Remove from the oven and nestle into the corner of a heavy ceramic serving bowl or cup. Put pecan halves on top. Next put Cola Red Onions next to it (warm them up beforehand). Put fresh cilantro on top of this. Slide the pickled burdock in at the edge, if you are using it. A little lemon juice may be added, if you like. The combined flavor as you mix and eat it together is something impossible to explain in words, which is undoubtedly why the monks named it this.

PICKLED BURDOCK ALTERNATIVE

Cut carrots into thin pieces about 10cm x 3mm x 3 mm (4 inches x 1/8 x 1/8 inch). Blanch in boiling salted water for 2 minutes. Then sprinkle with ground white pepper, MSG and rice vinegar. Refrigerate.

BEET LOAF

This is a dish worthy of a course in any Michelin star restaurant's vegetarian degustation menu, and is typical of the complexity involved in such fare. This was developed gradually over several years. The balance of the ingredients is crucial to its success, so measure carefully. Don't try to make an entire meal out of this because it is too potent in flavor. It should be a small individual course.

350g (12.3 oz)	Beets, cooked (see note below)
150g (5.3 oz)	Smoked Potatoes (page 124)
150g (5.3 oz)	Tomatoes, ripe
70g (2.5 oz)	Flour
60ml (2 oz)	Red Wine, dry
60g (2 oz)	Shallots, cut in thick slices
60g (2 oz)	Bread Crumbs
1 whole	Egg
25g (0.9 oz)	Date Syrup
1 T + 1/2 teaspoon	Deep Undertones Spice (page 142)
20ml (0.7 oz)	Olive Oil
8g (0.3 oz)	Parsley, fresh
1 teaspoon	Corn Starch
1/2 teaspoon	Salt

For serving: Horseradish and Sour Cream

THE BEETS

For the best method of cooking the beets, see page 172 of *Cooking in Russia, Volume 3.*

PROCEDURE

1. Cut the tomatoes into pieces so that they have a flat skin-side. Remove any heavy stems. This is the same method used for cutting the tomatoes as in the Gumbo video on YouTube.

2. Heat a skillet over a high heat (#8 out of 10). When it is hot, add the olive oil and wait a few seconds for it to get hot.

3. Add the tomatoes to the pan, skin-side down. Cook for about 4 minutes until the skin is blistered and starting to brown, but not burn.

4. Add the sliced shallots and the half teaspoon of salt to the pan and then reduce the heat slightly (#7). Cook with occasional stirring for about 4 more minutes.

5. Add the red wine and reduce the heat to medium-low (#4 out of 10). Reduce until it is a glaze, then remove the pan from the heat. This should also take about 4 minutes.

6. Chop the beets coarsely and put them in the bowl of a food processor along with the tomatoes and shallots from the pan (scrape in all the juices, too). Add the smoked potatoes, flour, bread crumbs, egg, date syrup, Deep Undertones Spice, parsley and corn starch.. Process to purée, scraping down the sides as necessary.

7. Ideally leave the mixture stand for 1-2 hours now, but this is not absolutely necessary.

8. Coat the bottom of a small ceramic loaf pan with a little olive oil. Put the mixture into the loaf pan and use a spatula to flatten out the top. Cover the top with a rectangle of parchment or baking paper cut to fit the space. Roast in a 160°C (320°F) oven with fan assist ON for 1 hour.

9. Remove the parchment (or baking paper) and return to the oven for another 15 minutes.

10. Leave out at room temperature for 2-3 hours before proceeding.

11. This is best served the next day. Cut thin "stained glass window" type slices and reheat briefly. Horseradish is essential. Blend with sour cream and pipe a floret at the edge of each plate.

BRICOLAGE SALAD

The vegetarian nouvelle Turkish sister of tuna salad. The magic here is the black tea and the poppy seeds that create flavor resonance (as explained in previous volumes of the Cooking in Russia series). This can be served by itself, or used as a filling for sandwiches.

300g (10.6 oz)	Zucchini
80g (2.8 oz)	Green Potato Gallimaufry (page 122)
30g (1 oz)	Walnuts, shelled
30g (1 oz)	Bread Crumbs
1 T	Poppy Seeds
1 1/2 teaspoons	Earl Gray Tea (out of a teabag is fine)
1 teaspoon	Fennel Seeds
1/2 teaspoon	Coarse Salt
1/2 teaspoon	MSG
22ml (0.75 oz)	Avocado Oil, or substitute Olive Oil
30g (1 oz)	Mayonnaise
30g (1 oz)	Avocado, diced
30g (1 oz)	Celery, finely diced
22g (0.75 oz)	Red Bell Pepper, finely diced
15g (0.5 oz)	Onion, finely diced
1 T	Parsley, freshly minced
1 teaspoon	Lemon Juice, fresh
Tomatoes, fresh vine-ripened	

PROCEDURE

1. Grind the walnuts in a food processor to small crumbs.

2. Grind the fennel seeds and coarse salt to a powder in an electric spice mill. The salt will help add mass and an abrasive to aid in the grinding.

3. Add the ground fennel seeds to the food processor along with the walnuts, bread crumbs, poppy seeds and tea. Process until as smooth as

possible.

4. Coarsely chop the zucchini. Put the chunks into a food processor. Grind until nearly a paste.

5. Heat a large nonstick skillet on a medium-high heat (#7 out of 10). When it is hot, add the olive oil. Swirl to bring the oil up to temperature, and then add the mixture from the food processor.

6. Stir frequently (but not constantly). Fry for about 15 minutes, being sure to cook evenly. Do not burn it by either increasing the heat or by cooking for much longer than 10 minutes.

7. Transfer to a bowl and let stand at room temperature about 30 minutes.

8. Chop the Green Potato Gallimaufry into small pieces.

8. When the zucchini has cooled stir together with the Green Potato Gallimaufry, the MSG, mayonnaise, avocado, celery, red bell pepper, onion, parsley and lemon juice. Refrigerate.

SOME APPLICATIONS

Slice tomatoes into thin wedges. Put a ring mold down on a plate and fill the bottom with overlapping tomato slices. Then use a spoon to fill most of the rest of the ring mold with the Bricolage Salad. Add another layer of tomatoes on top. Unmold and sprinkle with a little fresh parsley on top. Surround with small cubes of feta cheese and a drizzle of olive oil.

You can also put this in pita bread with lettuce and tomato. Pita bread will hold it together better.

If you are not a strict vegetarian, try stirring in some bay shrimp or crawfish tail meat. In that case, add a little more mayonnaise and lemon juice to balance the seafood—but it is still satisfying and delicious with just the vegetables.

FAUX BEEF STROGANOFF

There are many theories about the origin of this dish, but according to a Russian book published before the Soviet era, the dish was invented by a French chef employed by Count Pavel Stroganoff, which was a common arrangement at the time (see Volume 1 of Cooking in Russia). This dish has became known around the world in many different—and often almost unrecognizable forms—such as Shrimp Stroganoff in Brazil and Sausage Curry Stroganoff in Japan. The harmony of mushrooms with a rich sour cream gravy also happen to be ideal elements to conceal the aence of meat.

150g (5.3 oz)	Faux Ground Beef (page 96)
150g (5.3 oz)	Mushrooms, sliced
100ml (3.5 oz)	Red Wine, dry
60g (2 oz)	Sour Cream
35g (1.25 oz)	Butter
30g (1 oz)	Shallots, minced
15g (0.5 oz)	Garlic, minced
1 teaspoon	Novgorod Seasoning (see below)
1/2 teaspoon	Deep Undertones Spice (page 142)
1 T	Dill, fresh (or 1 teaspoon dry)
1/2 teaspoon	Parsley, dried
1/4 teaspoon	Black Pepper, ground

Pasta, preferably Fettuccine
Additional Butter and Sour Cream
Fresh Dill (for garnish)

NOVGOROD SEASONING

This is a complex spice mixture that requires cooking. The recipe is on page 237 of *Cooking in Russia, Volume 3*. You can replace it with 1/2 teaspoon of MSG, or leave it out completely and still have good results.

PROCEDURE

1. Heat a large nonstick skillet on medium-high (#7 out 10). Add the butter to the pan and wait until it foams up.

2. Add the sliced mushrooms to the pan and sprinkle with a little salt. Sauté for 3-4 minutes until they are soft.

3. Get a pan of lightly salted water boiling and begin cooking the pasta.

4. Reduce the heat to medium (#5 out of 10) and add the shallots and the garlic. Stir together for 2-3 minutes.

5. Scrape the contents of the pan off to a bowl. Increase the heat slightly (#6 out of 10) and add the Faux Ground Beef. Stir for 4-5 minutes to develop the full flavor.

6. Add the red wine and the Deep Undertones Spice. Stir together until it is mostly evaporated.

7. Add the mushroom mixture back to the pan and a ladle of the pasta water. Stir until very thick.

8. When the pasta is finished cooking, remove it to a bowl that contains some additional butter. The heat of the pasta will melt the butter, then toss to combine. This will flavor it and keep it from sticking to itself. Remember to save the pasta water since you will be using it.

9. Add another ladle of the pasta water and the dried dill, parsley, Novgorod Seasoning (or MSG) and black pepper. Stir until it is thick yet again.

10. Add the sour cream to the pan and stir. If it gets too thick, add a little more of the pasta water until it is completely cooked and you have the consistency desired.

11. Plate the pasta. Spoon over some of the sauce. Add another dollop of sour cream and a sprig of fresh dill to each plate. Alternatively you can mix more sour cream in the previous step, but it won't look as good when you plate it.

Sell your books at
World of Books!

Go to sell.worldofbooks.com
and get an instant price quote.
We even pay the shipping - see
what your old books are worth
today!

0008456862

8662 C-3

00084 56

Meat Substitutes

In addition to being the backbone of vegetarian dishes that simulate meat flavors, many of these can also be used as extenders for actual meat. Whether you are just trying to cut down on meat, or you have children who don't want to eat their vegetables, here's a way to take a little meat and a lot of vegetable and have it taste like a lot of meat with little or no vegetable. Below are some especially good blends. The balance between actual meat (if any) and the plant-based simulation is up to you, and once you try these, you'll see the advantage in taste and healthiness.

Faux Ground Beef	Ground Beef or Buffalo
Faux Dark Chicken	Ground Chicken (Breast or Dark Meat)
Carrot Farrago	Ground Pork or Venison
Cauliflower Caviar (without the mayonnaise)	Ground Turkey
Pomegranate Farrago	Ground Lamb or Duck
Soy Meat Substitute	Ground Veal
Red Onion Farrago	Ground Beef, Tuna Salad and Salmon Dishes

FAUX GROUND BEEF

By itself this is only vaguely similar to ground beef, but when used properly in a recipe it can be extremely convincing.

300g (10.6 oz)	Eggplant
30ml (1 oz)	Olive Oil
60g (2 oz)	Red Cargo Rice
50ml (1.75 oz)	Red Wine, dry
1 whole	Bay Leaf
1/2 teaspoon	Asafoetida (see note below)
15g (0.5 oz)	Pea Flour (peasemeal)
1 whole	Egg Yolk
3/4 teaspoon	Mediterranean Meat Spice (page 142)
90g (3 oz)	Tomato Purée (passata)
30ml (1 oz)	Vegetable Oil
3/4 teaspoon	Paprika

ASAFOETIDA

This is a spice usually seen in Indian cuisine (see Volume 2, page 35). You can leave it out, but I strongly encourage you to include it. It has a garlic-like flavor with the medicinal property of reducing stomach gas, which is important when consuming concentrated eggplant. Don't let the smell put you off because it changes dramatically after cooking.

PROCEDURE

1. Preheat oven to 210°C (410°F) - no fan assist. Trim the ends off the eggplant, then cut into 5mm (0.2 inch) slices, leaving the skin on.

2. Spread pieces out on a metal baking tray in a single layer. Use a pastry brush to paint each piece with the olive oil, leaving the down-facing side uncoated. Sprinkle with salt. Roast for 25 minutes.

3. While it is in the oven, put the rice into a sauce pan with the red wine. Bring to a rapid simmer and cook until just barely dry. Don't burn it.

5. Add 200ml (7 oz) water, the bay leaf and 1/2 teaspoon of salt. Bring to a simmer, then lower heat (#5 out of 10). Simmer for 10 minutes.

6. Now add the asafoetida to the rice. Reduce heat again (#3 out of 10) and cover. Cook for 30 minutes.

7. Turn the heat off and leave the lid on for at least 30 minutes.

8. Open and remove the bay leaf. If there is still liquid not absorbed, heat the pan again and cook until the excess liquid is gone.

9. When the time is up on the eggplant, turn the pieces over and return to the oven for 10 more minutes. Some pieces should be just starting to burn.

10. Cool the eggplant pieces until close to room temperature, then grind them in a food processor to large crumbs. Set aside.

11. Heat a nonreactive heavy sauce pan on high heat (#8 out of 10). When it is hot, add the vegetable oil to it. Allow a few seconds for it to get hot.

12. Have a splatter guard ready and add the tomato purée to the hot oil. Do not stir it. Cover with the splatter guard and wait 1 minute.

13. Add the paprika and reduce heat to medium (#5 out of 10). Do not stir for another minute.

14. Now add the eggplant from the food processor. Turn the heat off and cook with the residual heat for about 2 minutes.

15. Remove from the burner and wait about 5 minutes for it to cool.

16. Put the mixture into a food processor. Add the cooked rice, egg yolk, pea flour and Mediterranean Meat Spice. Grind to a hamburger-like consistency, scraping down the sides as necessary. Refrigerate for storage. This improves after being stored for 1-2 days.

USES

You can use this as you would ground beef in dishes where you would crumble the meat, such as Chilli con Carne, or as filling in a meat pie. Form into meatballs for pizza topping. Be sure the recipe you are using this with includes onion because onion is essential to the meat illusion.

SOY MEAT SUBSTITUTE

There are many commercial soy meat products marketed, but not with quality ingredients that make the difference.

120g (4 oz)	Soy Flour
80g (2.8 oz)	Kiwi fruit, peeled
45g (1.5 oz)	Mushrooms, cut into pieces
180ml (6.3 oz)	Mineral Watter, such as *Perrier*
20g (0.7 oz)	Pistachios, shelled
40g (1.4 oz)	Bread Crumbs
1 whole	Egg
3/4 teaspoon	Fennel Seeds
3/4 teaspoon	Pink Peppercorns
3/4 teaspoon	Coarse Salt

PROCEDURE

1. Blend the soy flour, kiwi fruit, mushrooms and water to a purée using a stick blender—or a regular blender if you are scaling this up.

2. Let the mixture stand at room temperature for about 45 minutes.

3. Grind the fennel seeds, pink peppercorns and salt to a powder and add it to the mixture along with the egg. Whisk together until smooth.

4. Heat a large nonstick skillet (with a good quality fresh nonstick coating) on a medium heat (#6 out of 10). Pour the mixture into the pan and spread it out evenly. Don't stir it.

5. Grind the pistachios and the bread crumbs together in a food processor until they are even crumbs. Sprinkle this on top of the mixture in the pan. Cook for about 6 minutes until there is a brown skin on the bottom.

6. Now mix it together and continue cooking another 6 minutes until you have a texture that's dry and crumbly very coarse meal. As with the Faux Ground Beef on the previous page, use this as if it were a raw ingredient.

IMPROVING TOFU

No vegetarian cookbook would be complete without tofu. However, tofu is one of the most commonly hated food products there is due to the texture and flavor. Here's how to fix it:

TEXTURE

Few people enjoy the chalky-spongy mouthfeel of tofu that was added directly to a sauce. Yet, that's exactly how many cooks use tofu. The easy solution is to coat it in corn starch and fry it first. Of course that only fixes the outside. If you cut pieces that are huge then the inside will still be squishy. Don't do that.

FLAVOR

Or rather the lack of flavor. Aside from unsalted rice cakes, tofu is the king of bland. Luckily, tofu is more porous than meat and so it absorbs marinades better. In fact, it absorbs marinades so well that you have to avoid highly acidic or salty pre-soaks or it can become too strongly flavored.

EXAMPLES FROM THIS BOOK

Tonkatsu is a popular Japanese dish of breaded pork and a special sauce. The tofu version here (page 143) is a good copy in both taste and texture. You can purchase Tonkatsu sauce in bottles in any Asian grocery store, or (far better) you can make your own using the video recipe on the *Cooking in Russia* YouTube channel, but that includes Worcestershire that is made from fish, in case you are a true vegetarian purist.

Fajitas is also a good approach to concealing the otherwise bland and squishy nature of tofu. See the recipe here on page (page 44).

FAUX DARK CHICKEN MEAT

This is very good simulation of chicken thigh and leg meat, provided that it is combined with other ingredients. Those with a very good palate will perceive it as dark chicken and mushrooms, but most people will not taste the mushrooms at all when it is in a finished dish.

450g (16 oz)	Button Mushrooms, fresh
70g (2.5 oz)	Onion
45g (1.5 oz)	Sourdough Bread, preferably stale
15ml (0.5 oz)	Sesame Oil (see note below)
15ml (0.5 oz)	Olive Oil, extra-virgin
1/4 (small piece)	Dried Green Serrano Chili Pepper
1 teaspoon	Coarse Salt
15g (0.5 oz)	Thyme, fresh branches

ADDITIONAL NOTES

Sesame oil comes in two types—light and dark (toasted). You want to use the toasted variety, which is usual type used in Asian cooking. If you find a bottle of sesame oil in an Asian market, it will almost certainly be the toasted type, even if it doesn't explicitly state that on the bottle. It is usually packaged in dark brown or opaque glass to protect it from light.

Don't substitute regular white bread for this, or another type of chili pepper if you want optimum results. Dried green serrano chilies are rarely seen for sale. You can make them yourself by oven drying fresh green ones at 80°C (150°F) overnight with fan assist ON in your oven.

PROCEDURE

1. Heat a pressure cooker on a medium-high setting (#7 out of 10). When it is hot, add the sesame and olive oil.

100

2. Cut the mushrooms in quarters and coarsely chop the onion and the sourdough bread. Add these to the pan when the oil is hot. Stir occasionally for about 6 minutes.

3. During this time, put the dried green chili and the coarse salt in an electric spice mill and grind to a powder. The salt works as an abrasive. You need a little bit to create chicken flavor, but

4. When the 6 minutes have elapsed, add the salt and green chili to the mushroom mixture and lower the heat to medium (#5 out of 10). Cook another 2-3 minutes.

5. Tie a string around the thyme branches to make them easier to remove as a single piece. Add 150ml (5.3 oz) water to the pressure cooker. Stir and then place the thyme bundle on top. Put the lid on the pressure cooker and increase the heat to medium-high (#7 out of 10) to get up to pressure.

6. Now reduce the heat to low (#2 to 3 out of 10 and begin counting 30 minutes.

7. Turn off the heat. Cool for a couple of minutes before releasing the pressure. Remove the thyme. If there is a puddle of liquid at the bottom, then turn the heat back up to medium (#5 out of 10) and cook until it is almost dry. Transfer to a bowl to cool completely.

OTHER TYPES OF MUSHROOMS

Ordinary button mushrooms, also known as champignons, have the least natural mushroom flavor, so they are what you should choose unless you actually *want* to emphasize the mushrooms. If that's an advantage for your application, then chanterelles are a good choice for a pleasant balance. If you use a strong tasting variety, then mushrooms are all you will taste.

EGGPLANT SALAMI

The look of this is almost a perfect copy of salami if you do it right. The flavor is quite good as long as it is combined with other ingredients. The initial bite is not the same, but the midrange and aftertaste are a good simulation, so you can make this work well by combining it in dishes where other elements dominate the initial taste. If you don't have a stove top smoker, you can add liquid smoke to the oil, but the results won't be as good.

150g (5.3 oz)	Eggplant, peeled and sliced 3mm (1/8")
1 T + 1 teaspoon	Hidden Salami seasoning (page 141)
60ml (2 oz)	Olive Oil
1/4 teaspoon	Red Food Coloring
1 T	Wood Chips, preferably apple wood

PROCEDURE

1. Combine the spice mixture with the oil and the food coloring in a small bowl. Use a silicone brush to mix them together.

2. Lay the round slices of eggplant out on a metal cookie sheet (don't use a silicone mat). Paint each slice with the mixture.

3. Turn the pieces over and use what's left of the mixture to paint the other side. The second side should get much less than the first side did.

4. Turn the pieces back over again so that the more heavily painted side is facing up. Preheat the oven to 170°C (340°F) with the broiler supplying the heat and fan assist ON. Place on a shelf 25cm (10 inches) from the heat source. Roast for approximately 11 minutes. However broilers vary, so you may need to adjust the timing. It is important that it is very well cooked at this stage, or the simulation will fail.

5. Remove the eggplant slices with tweezers and drain on paper towels.

6. Set up a stove top smoker with the wood chips. Put the eggplant slices into the smoker. The edges can overlap. Put the smoker on a burner set to maximum heat (#10 out of 10) with the lid cracked open and wait until the first wisps of smoke appear.

7. Close the lid and reduce the heat to medium-high (#7 out of 10). Smoke for 2 minutes.

8. Move the smoker off of the heat but keep it closed for 2 more minutes.

9. Transfer the eggplant slices onto a large platter in a single layer. Sprinkle with finely ground salt and black pepper. Put the plate in the refrigerator with no cover for 1 hour. This will take the harsh edge off of the smoke. Then transfer to a sealed storage container and keep in the refrigerator until needed.

SANDWICHES

You can make a sandwich with this that is quite convincing if you include all the trimmings (cheese, mustard, mayonnaise, lettuce, tomato, onion and pickles). Fry the Eggplant Salami briefly first for better results.

BREAKFAST HOUSE HASH

150g (5.3 oz)	Potatoes, peeled and coarsely chopped
75g (2.6 oz)	Onion
45g (1.5 oz)	Eggplant Salami
3/4 teaspoon	Thyme, dried
40g (1.4 oz)	Butter

Grind potatos, onion, Eggplant Salami and thyme together in a food processor. Heat a nonstick skillet on medium and add the butter. When it foams up, add the mix from the food processor. Cover with a lid and cook about 10 minutes, lifting to stir only occasionally. When it is becoming crisp, remove the lid and cook until almost dry. Add salt and fresh ground pepper. Can be reheated. This is a great breakfast item with toast and eggs.

FAUX SEAFOOD

The taste is that of a mixture of seafood. You seem to taste shrimp, octopus, clams and some vague related seafood flavors.

300ml (10.6 oz)	Beer, light lager (see note below)
90g (3 oz)	Oatmeal, parboiled - unsweetened plain
60g (2 oz)	Okra, previously frozen (thawed)
30g (1 oz)	Mushrooms, preferably Chanterelles
20g (0.7 oz)	Butter
1 teaspoon	Salt
1 teaspoon	MSG
1/4 teaspoon	Asafoetida
30g (1 oz)	Bread Crumbs
2 whole	Eggs, medium (or 1 1/2 extra large)

ADDITIONAL INFORMATION

The oatmeal called for is the type that cooks in 3 to 5 minutes. Don't use the truly instant one that cooks just on the addition of hot water.

The success of this recipe depends on both the beer and the MSG. The final dish will not contain any measurable amount of alcohol, and I have already written extensively about the safety of MSG (see page 10-11).

Singapore Tiger beer is an excellent choice if you can get it. The key is that it won't be bitter on reduction or overpower with malt or hops.

PROCEDURE

1. Chop the mushrooms and the okra into small pieces.

2. In a 2-liter sauce pan, combine the oatmeal, beer, okra, mushrooms, butter, salt, and asafoetida. Heat on medium-high (#7 out of 10) until it comes to a simmer. Stir frequently during this time.

3. Now reduce the heat a bit (#5-6 out of 10). Continue stirring occasionally (not constantly) for about 20 minutes. The aroma of the asafoetida will gradually fade during this time.

4. Stir in the bread crumbs. Continue cooking about 10 more minutes until the mixture is coarse, crumbly and slightly toasty but not in any way burnt.

5. Stir in the MSG and remove from the heat to cool.

6. Cover with cling film and refrigerate for at least an hour.

7. Blend with the eggs to form a homogeneous paste.

8. Divide mixture onto two large squares of cling film. Roll them up like large sausages. Either tie the ends with string, or spin the film around so that it knots itself. Now wrap this up in foil, folding and crimping the ends. Now wrap that package up in a second layer of foil.

9. Fill a pot with enough water to hold the sausage-like packets. Bring to a rapid simmer (but not a rolling boil). Now put in the packets. Reduce heat as needed to maintain a simmer (not a boil) for 20 minutes.

10. Remove the packets, but don't open them. Leave at room temperature for 30-60 minutes, then transfer to the refrigerator for several hours until completely chilled.

11. Now you can open the packets. Discard the foil and cling film to reveal logs that you can slice.

FRIED FISH CAKE VARIATION

Follow the above procedure up to step #7. Form patties instead and fry on a nonstick pan in a little olive oil until golden brown on each side. Serve with a mayonnaise or garlic aioili, or a sauce of your choosing.

FAUX FRIED FISH FILLETS

Although the preparation is a little work, you will end up with several faux fish fillets that you can store in your refrigerator and use for recipes in the days that follow. In many classic fish recipes, the fish is floured and fried as part of the preparation, producing a crust on the fish. This simulates that stage, so you do not need to fry these a second time when using them in fish recipes. Simply warm them back up in the sauce. Of course the simulation is not perfect, but it does provide a way to make a satisfying meal that contains no actual meat (or fish, of course).

180g (6.3 oz)	Zucchini, fresh
90g (3 oz)	Quinoa
15g (0.5 oz)	Maasdam or Swiss Cheese
1 T	Soy Flour
2 teaspoons	Fennel Salt (see below)
1/4 teaspoon	Turmeric
300ml (10.6 oz)	*Donat Mg* Mineral Water (see below)
1 whole	Egg
about 2 T	Olive Oil (in all)

ADDITIONAL INFORMATION

Quinoa is a grain. You can substitute polenta, but then it will have a corn flavor that will not taste nearly as fish-like.

Donat Mg is a mineral water from Slovenia that has a faint fish-like aroma. It is widely available in Europe, though may be difficult to find in America and Asia. You can substitute Perrier or some other mineral water, but the result will not be as good.

The procedure for making Fennel Salt is on page 21 of *Cooking in Russia, Volume 3*. You can substitute 1 teaspoon of ordinary table salt.

PROCEDURE

1. Chop the zucchini coarsely and put it into a blender with the soy flour, cheese, turmeric, a teaspoon of the olive oil, and 200ml (7 oz) of the mineral water. Purée.

2. Transfer the contents to a sauce pan and bring to a simmer on a medium heat (#5 to 6 out of 10). Maintain at a simmer for 10 minutes.

3. Stir in the quinoa. Reduce heat (#3 out of 10) and cover for 15 minutes.

4. Add the fennel salt and rest of the mineral water. Increase heat to medium (#6 out of 10). Stir until it is dough-like in consistency.

5. Transfer to a bowl to cool at room temperature for 5-6 minutes.

6. Mix in the egg. Now refrigerate the mixture for at least 30 minutes.

7. Lightly brush the bottom of a baking tray with olive oil. Spread the mixture out into fish-like shapes onto the oil-coated sheet. You can work in batches to make this easier. Add a little more olive oil on top of each piece and then use a rubber spatula to smooth the tops. Each one should be about 6.5mm high (1/4 inch) and whatever shape you like. Use the spatula to square up the sides, too.

8. Preheat your broiler to 160°C (320°F). Put the baking sheet on a rack positioned 15cm (6 inches) from the broiler heating element. Broil for about 10 minutes, but broilers vary so keep an eye on it. You want it to have a golden brown color on top.

9. Remove from the oven and allow to cool for about 10 minutes before you remove each piece with a fish spatula to a plate for holding, taking care not to break the pieces.

Note that they are still undercooked. This is by design so that you can place them into a skillet to reheat at the same time you add any sauce. If you want to eat them directly, then heat some oil in a pan and fry on both sides until golden brown. These must have a citrus component to be deceptive - lime or lemon. You can serve with tartar sauce or ketchup and lemon, or go the extra step and try the Piccata Pan Sauce (page 129).

CARROT FARRAGO

Long ago the term "mincemeat" (as in Mincemeat Pie) meant a mixture of venison or pork with spices and some fruit such as raisins. Over time and periods of poverty, the meat was left out. Although this is vegetarian and doesn't actually contain raisins, it is reminiscent of 19th century venison mincemeat.

300g (10.6 oz)	Carrots, peeled
90g (3.2 oz)	Red Onion, diced
90g (3.2 oz)	White Beans, canned
22g (0.75 oz)	Pomegranate Molasses
30ml (1 oz)	Peanut Oil
2 whole	Bay Leaves, dried Turkish
1 teaspoon	Thyme, dried
1 teaspoon	Coarse Salt
3/4 teaspoon	Cumin Seeds
1/2 teaspoon	White Peppercorns (or ground)
1/2 teaspoon	Ginger, ground

POMEGRANATE MOLASSES

Do not substitute pomegranate juice or ordinary sugar molasses. Both are completely different. Pomegranate molasses is available in any Middle Eastern, Greek or Russian specialty grocery store, or online. It is an essential ingredient in many cuisines, but seldom seen in European or American recipes.

PROCEDURE

1. Cut the carrots into 8cm (about 1/3 inch) dice.

2. Heat a large skillet on medium-high (#7 out of 10). When it is hot, add the peanut oil and swirl to coat the bottom of the pan evenly. When the oil is hot, add the cubed carrot. Arrange the pieces in a single layer so that

they are all in direct contact with the pan.

3. Now begin to count the time. Cook for 8 minutes without stirring.

3. Stir and then cook for another 3 minutes without stirring further.

4. Continue cooking now with occasional stirring until the carrots are darker and there is the aroma of caramelization.

5. Add the diced red onion to the pan and lower the heat to medium (#5 out of 10). Cook until the onion is soft, which should be about 2 minutes.

6. Remove the pan from the heat and add the white beans. Cook using the residual heat. Then set aside to cool for a few minutes before proceeding.

7. Grind the cumin seeds with the thyme, white pepper, coarse salt and ground ginger in an electric spice mill. Alternatively, if you are using ground cumin and ground white pepper, you don't need to grind the spices but the best results are obtained with whole spices that are freshly ground.

8. Put the cooled carrot mixture into a food processor. Add the pomegranate molasses and the spices. Grind to coarse meal. Don't purée.

9. Scrape the mixture into a metal pan as explained for the Broise method (page 26). Push the two bay leaves down into the mixture, equidistant from the center. Cover tightly with foil. Place on a shelf 15cm (6 inches) from the broiler element in a 170°C (340°F) preheated oven for 30 minutes.

10. Remove the tray from the oven and let stand at room temperature for at least 15 minutes before you open it. Remove and discard the bay leaves. Then transfer to a container and refrigerate.

APPLICATIONS

In addition to the recipes in this book that call for this, try using this as a filling in puff pastry pies. You can also try combining this with the Faux Ground Beef (page 96) to enhance the meatiness.

GREEN FARRAGO

Among the Farrago series, this one lets the vegetable flavor shine through more, but it's still dense and satisfying. You can scale this up easily by just multiplying all of the ingredients. Remember to use a shallow pan for the Broise cooking, regardless of what length and width it may be.

150g (5.3 oz)	Green Beans, previously frozen is okay
50g (1.75 oz)	Arugula (also known as Rocket)
50g (1.75 oz)	Spinach, frozen (see below)
15g (0.5 oz)	Bread Crumbs
1 T	Olive Oil
1 teaspoon	Lemon Juice, fresh
1 clove	Garlic, peeled
2 whole	Bay Leaves
1 teaspoon	Corn Starch
1/2 teaspoon	Paprika
1/2 teaspoon	Green Peppercorns, dried
1/2 teaspoon	Basil, dried
1/2 teaspoon	Coarse Salt
1/8 teaspoon	Nutmeg, ground

SPINACH

You can substitute 30g (1 ounce) of fresh spinach for the frozen, if you prefer. The results will be indistinguishable.

PROCEDURE

1. Whether you are using frozen or fresh green beans, first boil them in lightly salted water until just cooked.

2. Remove the green beans from the water with a slotted spoon or spider, then put the spinach into the same water. Cook until just done, then remove and set that aside, too.

3. Pick any large stems off of the arugula, then put it in a bowl. Toss with the corn starch.

4. Combine the olive oil with the lemon juice. Add this to the arugula and mix well. Spread out on a metal baking sheet.

5. Put the arugula in a preheated 130°C (265°F) oven with fan assist ON for 20 to 25 minutes.

6. During this time, mince the garlic and crush the green peppercorns in a mortar with the coarse salt.

7. Remove the arugula from the oven and scrape off the baking sheet. It should be dry and crumbly. Put this into the bowl of a food processor along with the green beans, spinach, bread crumbs, minced garlic, paprika, basil, nutmeg, green peppercorns and salt. Grind together until it is coarse meal consistency.

8. Scrape into a shallow metal baking tray as explained for the Broise Method (page 26). Stick the bay leaves into the mixture equidistant from the edges. Cover in foil.

9. Roast at 170°C (340°F) for 30 minutes.

10. Remove from the oven and let stand at room temperature for 10-15 minutes before opening. Discard the bay leaves. Yield is about 180 grams.

SIMPLE APPLICATIONS

Mix 1 part of minced leek (white part only) with 6 parts of Green Farrago and 8 parts of chopped freshly steamed (or boiled) broccoli, a small amount of sour cream and salt (to taste) for a delicious vegetable side dish, or a vegetarian degustation course that can be plated with the aid of a ring mold and a little imagination. It's also nice for picnics.

If you like spicy food, mix this with diced jalapeño chiles and cheddar cheese as a filling for the Stuffed Buns (page 74)

RED ONION FARRAGO

Here is another taste illusion facilitated by an unlikely combination of ingredients. The carrots and the lingonberries add complexity while simultaneously softening the red onion. The net result adds background meatiness as an ingredient.

300g (10.6 oz)	Red Onions, peeled
150g (5.3 oz)	Carrots, peeled
80g (2.8 oz)	Lingonberries, previously frozen and thawed
25ml (0.9 oz)	Olive Oil
22g (0.75 oz)	Garlic cloves, peeled
2-3 sprigs	Cilantro
2 teaspoons	Deep Undertones Spice (page 142)
2 teaspoons	Balsamic Vinegar (see page 25)
1 teaspoon	Salt
1/4 teaspoon	MSG

PROCEDURE

1. Coarsely chop the red onion and garlic. Put these into a food processor with the thawed lingonberries. Grind to coarse meal.

2. Scrape out the contents of the food processor bowl to a shallow metal dish, as explained for the Broise method (page 26). Place the cilantro on top of the onion mixture, then seal with heavy foil.

3. Preheat broiler to 170°C (340°F) and position the shelf 15cm (6 inches) from the heat source.

4. Cook the mixture for 60 minutes. During this time, peel the carrots and cut them into brunois (about 3mm or 1/8" dice). Don't obsess about them being perfectly cut. If some are a bit smaller or larger it won't matter in the end.

5. Remove the tray from the oven when the time is up and allow to stand for 15 more minutes before opening it. During this time heat a large

nonstick skillet on a medium heat (#6 out of 10). Add the olive oil to the pan when it is hot and allow a minute for the oil to get hot.

6. Add the diced carrot to the pan. Stir initially to get the carrot pieces evenly coated with the oil, and then don't stir for about 12 minutes.

7. Now you can remove the foil from the pan that was under the broiler. Discard the sprigs of cilantro on top.

8. When the 12 minutes of time is up on the carrots, add the contents from the pan that was under the broiler. Stir while continuing to cook for 5-6 minutes.

9. Add the Deep Undertones Spice and the salt. Continue stirring and cooking for another 5-6 minutes.

10. Transfer to a bowl and cool for a few minutes. Add the Balsamic vinegar and the MSG. Stir to combine evenly. Refrigerate for several hours to give the flavors a chance to soften. You may need to return it to the food processor if you need a fine texture for a particular application.

SAMPLE APPLICATIONS

Mince together a little "salad" of roughly equal parts of cilantro and scallions. Put a portion of the Red Onion Farrago down on a plate using a small ring mold. Add a twist of black pepper. Top this with the cilantro and scallion. This is ideal as an amuse bouche, or a single course of a degustation. Originally this was paired with seafood in a roasted tomatillo butter sauce.

Another interesting (non-vegetarian) application for this is to combine it with tuna salad. You can make it up to 50% by weight of Red Onion Farrago and then add a little more mayonnaise. It is delicious, even more economical, and much higher in fiber and other nutrients.

POMEGRANATE FARRAGO

This is an outstanding vegetarian ravioli filling. It has an ethereal protein taste that defies description. The flavors change as you chew each bite. Be sure to try the recipe for the amazing Vegetarian Reuben Sandwich on page 47.

280g (9.9 oz)	Carrots, peeled
180g (6.3 oz)	Pomegranate pulp, fresh
140g (4.9 oz)	White Beans, canned
75g (2.6 oz)	Red Onion, peeled
20ml (0.7 oz)	Olive Oil, extra-virgin
15ml (1 T)	Balsamic Vinegar (see page 25)
2 teaspoons	Summer Savory, dried (see below)
2 teaspoons	Cumin Seeds
1 teaspoon	Coarse Salt
3/4 teaspoon	White Peppercorns
1 clove	Garlic, chopped
1/2 teaspoon	Liquid Smoke

SUMMER SAVORY

This herb can be difficult to find. The recipe will still work okay if you use a commercial blend of French herbs, which usually contain savory.

PROCEDURE

1. Put the summer savory, cumin seeds, white peppercorns and coarse salt into an electric spice mill and grind to a powder.

2. Drain and rinse the white beans.

3. Tamp out the seed pockets from the pomegranate, taking care to discard any large white fibrous membranes.

4. Coarsely chop the carrots and red onion. Put these into a food processor and add all of the other ingredients. Run the machine until the

mixture is finely minced. This will take about a full minute.

5. Spread the mixture onto an ovenproof metal dish as previously explained for Broise cooking (page 26). Cover with parchment paper, and then seal the top over with foil.

6. Roast at 160°C (320°F) for 1 hour and 20 minutes.

7. Remove from the oven, but leave the cover on for another 15 minutes.

8. Pass the mixture through a food mill using the medium perforated disc. The coarse disc will allow pomegranate seeds through, and the fine will not permit much material to pass through at all. Expect that it will take some effort to get most of the material through the mill and that you will have a substantial portion of solids that will not pass through due mostly to the pomegranate seeds. Be sure to scrape the bottom of the perforated plate, too. Yield is about 400 grams (14 ounces). If it is much less, then you aren't done, so go back and crank the food mill some more. Discard the solids, or add them to your compost heap if you have one.

9. Cover with cling film and chill down in the refrigerator overnight or longer before use. The flavors must have a chance to mellow and blend.

POMEGRANATE SALMAGUNDI

To convert the Pomegranate Farrago to Pomegranate Salmagundi, the proportional ingredients are as follows (multiply everything to scale up):

120g (4 oz)	Pomegranate Farrago
2 whole	Hard Boiled Eggs, peeled and chopped
1 1/2 T	Shallot, minced
1 teaspoon	Lemon Juice, freshly squeezed
1/4 teaspoon	Sage, dried (or 3/4 teaspoon fresh)
1/4 teaspoon	MSG

Mash all of the ingredients together with the back of a fork until as smooth as possible. Serve either cold or warm with bread and butter.

(continued on next page)

POMEGRANATE FARRAGO (continued)

Another application for Pomegranate Farrago is with the plugs you take out making the *Zucchini Filets with Goat Cheese* (page 66). Toss these with corn starch and then deep fry for a couple of minutes to crisp up the outside. Set them aside to drain on paper towel. In a skillet, fry some shallots and garlic in a little vegetable oil. When the shallots are turning golden, add some of the Pomegranate Farrago and an equal portion of puréed tomatoes (passata). Fry together for 3-4 minutes, then add the deep fried zucchini cylinders to the pan. The exact quantity of these ingredients is up to you. Toss to combine well and cook just until the zucchini starts to melt a bit, in spite of the fried coating. Serve with freshly chopped scallions on top and bread or toast on the side.

RAVIOLI FILLING

As previously mentioned, the Pomegranate Farrago makes a great ravioli filling. Just combine some with fine bread crumbs and grated Parmigianino-Reggiano cheese for body, mouthfeel and balance.

Other Preparations

There are usually more steps involved in using fruits and vegetables to simulate meat than in just cooking some meat, as you would reasonably expect. Fruits, vegetables and starches don't just taste like meat on their own. Most dishes require at least two layers of manipulation, with the first one being the production of the basic underlying flavors using natural non-meat ingredients. The preparations in this section are some common fundamental methods that you will find generally useful.

The good news is that all of these preparations have a long shelf life in the refrigerator. Some are a bit finicky to make, but at least you won't have to make them every time you are working on one of the other recipes in this book that calls for them. You can scale all of these up just by multiplying the ingredient quantities.

I've recently discovered just how delicious plants can be if you know how to cook them right.

That's right. Now I'm a vegetarian!

Of course being a vegetarian doesn't mean I'm a pacifist!

So the difference is that now you don't eat what you kill?

I'm not a monster.

VEGETABLE BROTH

The balance has been selected to compliment the recipes in this book. Although there is a teaspoon of salt, which is not used in stocks, it is important for breaking down the vegetables, and it can still be considered low sodium given the total volume.

240g (8.5 oz)	Butternut Squash, raw (skin-on is okay)
140g (4.9 oz)	Onion, peeled
120g (4.2 oz)	Carrots, peeled
100g (3.5 oz)	Celery
50g (1.8 oz)	Bell Pepper, preferably red
25ml (0.9 oz)	Olive Oil, extra-virgin
2-3 cloves	Garlic
2-3 branches	Thyme, fresh
1/2 teaspoon	Black Peppercorns
1 whole	Bay Leaf
1/4 teaspoon	Cloves, whole (the spice)
1 teaspoon	Salt

PROCEDURE

1. Coarsely chop the squash, onion, carrot, celery and bell pepper.

2. Heat a pressure cooker on high (#8 out of 10). When hot, add the oil.

3. When the oil is hot, fry the onion pieces for 2 minutes until browning.

4. Add the other chopped vegetables and the salt. Cook with occasional stirring for 10 minutes.

5. Now add the garlic, thyme, black peppercorns, bay leaf and cloves. Stir and then add 1.2 liters (42 ounces) of water. When it starts to come to a simmer, reduce the heat to low (#3 out of 10) and put the lid on it.

6. Maintain pressure just below the venting point for one hour.

7. Let cool for another hour before opening. Pass through a sieve.

CARROT COMESTIBLE

This deceptively simple mixture tastes like a jigsaw puzzle of savory meat flavors that are trying to be assembled about 15 seconds after you taste it. You can easily see how this can be used to bolster meat simulations with structure and depth.

200g (7 oz)	Carrots
45ml (1.5 oz)	Vegetable Oil
22g (0.75 oz)	Garlic cloves, peeled
1 1/2 teaspoons	Hidden Salami Spice (page 141)
2-3 whole	Turkish Bay Leaves, dried

PROCEDURE

1. Peel the carrots and cut them into large pieces. Boil in salted water for until soft (about 15 minutes). Drain. The weight is measured after boiling.

2. Combine the carrots and all of the other ingredients except the bay leaves in a food processor. Grind to an even consistency.

3. Heat a large nonstick skillet on high (#8 out of 10). When it is hot, add the mixture along with the bay leaves. Listen for when it starts to sizzle.

4. After a minute of sizzling, lower the heat to medium (#6 out of 10). Stir frequently and cook for about 20 minutes. During the last 2-3 minutes of the cooking time as most of the water has been driven off, the temperature will start to rise, it will darken slightly and the aroma will change.

5. Discard the bay leaves. Transfer the mixture to a bowl to cool. If you did this correctly, you should have just over 100 grams (3.5 ounces) of product. The "soul mate" of this Blackwood Rice (page 121). The two go together in an almost magical way.

COLA RED ONIONS

This is a sort of an onion version of sweet and sour cabbage that is a great accompaniment to vegetables grilled over coals.

450g (15.9 oz)	Red Onions, cut into rings
45g (1.5 oz)	Vegetable Oil
200ml (7 oz)	Coca-Cola (in all)
100g (3.5 oz)	Tomatoes, diced
1 T	Red WIne Vinegar
1 whole	Bay Leaf
1/2 teaspoon	Paprika

COCA-COLA

Although you can use the internationally famous brand, better results will be obtained using Afri-Cola from Germany.

PROCEDURE

1. Heat a very large nonstick skillet on a medium setting (#6 out of 10). Add the oil to the pan when it is hot. Now add the diced tomatoes, skin-side down. Cook without moving the tomatoes until they are blistered.

2. Remove the tomatoes to a bowl and then add the rest of the oil followed by the red onions and the bay leaf. Cook for 3 minutes.

3. Add a third of the cola and cook for about 12 minutes until thick.

4. Add another third of the cola and 1 1/2 teaspoons of salt. Continue cooking down to a glaze again.

5. Add the rest of the cola and the paprika. Reduce until almost dry.

6. Return the tomatoes to the pan and the vinegar. Turn the heat down a little (#5 out of 10). Cover and cook for 5-6 minutes.

7. Remove the lid and cook until almost dry again.

BLACKWOOD RICE

Deep and dark, this is an outstanding ingredient to base a faux meat dish on. The tomato paste can be either the Italian high quality type in a tube, or prepared according to Volume 3.

100g (3.5 oz)	Brown Rice
45g (1.5 oz)	Tomato Paste, quality Italian type
30ml (1 oz)	Red Wine, dry
1 teaspoon	Cocoa powder, unsweetened
1 teaspoon	Orange Zest, freshly grated
3/4 teaspoon	Paprika
1/2 teaspoon	Garlic Powder
1/2 teaspoon	Oregano, dried
250ml (8.8 oz)	Water

PROCEDURE

1. Combine all of the ingredients except the wine in a sauce pan.

2. Bring to a good simmer on a medium-high heat (#7 out of 10). Continue cooking with some stirring for about 15 minutes until thickened.

3. Stir in the red wine. Put a lid on the pan and reduce the heat to low (#3 out of 10). Cook for 30 minutes without disturbing the contents.

4. Reduce the heat further to very low (#1 out of 10). Leave the lid on and continue cooking for another 20 minutes.

5. Turn the heat off and allow it to stand without opening it for 15 more minutes. If there is still liquid, then turn the heat on and reduce until dry.

6. Open and transfer to a bowl to cool. The rice is still not fully cooked, because it is expected you will use this in an application where it will be cooked more. The yield is about 300 grams (10.6 oz).

GREEN POTATO GALLIMAUFRY

This contributes both savory flavor and texture (otherwise known as mouthfeel) when trying to simulate meat, as well as being an interesting side dish or plating element on its own.

250g (8.8 oz)	Potatoes, peeled
45g (1.5 oz)	Spinach, fresh
15g (0.5 oz)	Cheddar Cheese, grated
15ml (0.5 ml)	Gin (see note below)
15ml (0.5 ml)	Olive Oil
10g (0.3 oz)	Capers, rinsed
1 teaspoon	Chives, dried
1/2 teaspoon	Salt

THE GIN

The alcohol in the gin will extract flavors that you can't get with water (see *Cooking in Russia, Volume 3*). It also adds a lot of herbal notes. However, if you are firmly opposed to using alcohol, then substitute water.

PROCEDURE

1. Put the spinach, grated cheddar, gin, olive oil, capers, chives and salt into the cup of a stick blender and purée.
2. Slice the potatoes on a mandolin set to 1.3mm (0.05 inches).
3. Mix the potato slices in a bowl with the purée from the stick blender cup. Use your fingers to make sure every slice of potato is coated.
4. Put a silicone mat (Silpat) down on a baking sheet and spread the potatoes out in a single layer across the surface. If your oven is small, then do this in two batches. Make sure the potatoes do not overlap. There will be additional liquid in the bowl. Drizzle this over the potatoes. If you are working in two batches, then divide the extra liquid in half for each part.

5. Cook in a preheated broiler at 180°C (355°F) about 10cm (4 inches) from the heating element with fan assist ON for about 11-12 minutes, however broilers vary so keep a careful watch the first time. The edges of the potatoes should be browned when you are done, but <u>not</u> burnt.

6. Remove from the oven and allow to rest undisturbed at room temperature for at least 15 minutes so that the residual heat will assist in evaporating more moisture. There will still be some slightly damp parts and some bone dry very crisp parts. This is normal. The dry parts will absorb the moisture from the wetter parts after being stored for a while, since most applications will involve grinding this up in a food processor with other ingredients. If you are not using it immediately, store it in a sealed container in the refrigerator.

SOME SAMPLE APPLICATIONS

Combine (by weight) 3 parts of the Faux Dark Chicken (page 100) with 1 part of this Green Potato Gallimaufry in a food processor to create a very flavorful meat substitute that you can...

- Mix with cheese to stuff tomatoes for baking.
- Mix with rice as the filling for stuffed bell peppers.
- Mix with peas and carrots and Béchamel as a pot pie filling.

Once you taste this combination, you'll see how this can be used in many different recipes.

SMOKED POTATOES

A load of smokey goodness and body that can be added to dishes, or just toss with a little sea salt and seasoning such as minced rosemary and garlic for a delicious side dish or snack.

450g (16 oz)	Potatoes (see note below)
1 T	Salt
1 T	Olive Oil
2 teaspoons	Wood Chips, ideally Mesquite

TYPE OF POTATOES

You want a potato that is neither starchy or waxy—something in between. While 8 minutes boiling is average, your potatoes may vary.

PROCEDURE

1. Peel the potatoes and cut them up into cubes about 4cm (1.6 inches).
2. Put them in a pot and add enough water to cover them by about 2cm (0.8 inches). Add the salt to the water and bring to a boil.
3. After the boiling has started, begin counting about 8 minutes of time.
4. Drain on a colander, then transfer to a bowl. Toss with the olive oil, then return to the colander to stand at room temperature for an hour or so.
5. Load a stove top smoker with the wood chips. Arrange the potato cubes on the wire rack inside of it. Close the lid except for a small crack and begin heating on your highest stove setting.
6. As soon as smoke begins to drift out of the opening, close the lid the rest of the way and reduce the stove heat to medium (#5 out of 10). Smoke for 20 minutes, then remove the smoker from the burner element and let it cool at room temperature for 10 minutes before you open it up.

✦

CHINESE DRAGON CABBAGE

This slightly bitter product will add another dimension of meat or fish flavor in a surprising way. The cabbage is traditionally toasted outdoors slowly near a smoky fire—which is where the reference to (fire breathing) dragons came from. If you can roast it that way, then it will be even more flavorful.

60g (2 oz)	Chinese Cabbage or Napa Cabbage
1 teaspoon	Corn Starch
1/2 teaspoon	Salt
1 T	Vegetable Oil

PROCEDURE

1. Trim the cabbage so that there are no tough fibry stems. You want only the tender leaves. The measured weight is just the leaves.

2. Put the leaves in a bowl and add the corn starch. Toss to coat evenly.

3. Add the vegetable oil and toss to mix again.

4. Preheat oven to 170°C (340·F). Spread the mixture out on a metal baking sheet.

4. When the oven is hot, switch the broiler on. Position a shelf 15cm (6 inches) from the heating element. Put the baking sheet in the oven for about 10 minutes. The time will vary with broilers. The cabbage leaves should be quite brown and almost completely dry, but not actually burnt. Now remove them and toss with the salt.

5. When they have cooled completely, crumble them and store at room temperature. You can put it in a glass jar as you would a spice and it will keep for at least a week.

Sauces

Sauces are a fundamental part of almost every cuisine around the world in some form or another, even if it is just mustard on a hot dog. A well crafted sauce offers a way to blanket food in an unctuous and highly flavorful coating. A sauce can either smooth sharp flavors with butter, cream and cheese, or sharpen mild flavors with vinegar, citrus and chilies. Sauces can also mask defects, as every child who has poured ketchup over Mom's reheated leftovers to try and make it palatable knows. When it comes to trying to imitate meat using plant matter, sauces are one of your most potent tools to blur the details like a magician working behind a translucent curtain. You know there's some trickery afoot, but a sauce can make it more convincing, even if it is only as a means of distraction.

BÉCHAMEL SAUCE

The most fundamental sauce that every cook needs to be a master of is Béchamel. Although the name includes the word "sauce", it is seldom used directly as a sauce. Rather, it is a building block to more complex sauces such as the Aurora Sauce here (page 132). When using the Farrago series and other preparations here to forge your own creations, keep a sauce in mind, and you can build a vast number of sauces just from Béchamel and simple ingredients. One very good example is by combining Béchamel Sauce with a little black truffle oil (or black truffles) and the Super Tapenade from page 206 of Cooking in Russia, Volume 3.

Many books tell you to use scalded milk (milk that has been boiled briefly first), but this is a leftover mistake from long ago that many cooks have been blindly following because they don't know the science or the history. Before the days when milk was pasteurized, it still contained active enzymes that interfered with the formation of the Béchamel. So the milk was boiled first to denature those enzymes. Unless you are actually using unpasteurized milk, there is no reason boil it first.

The standard method of preparing a Béchamel Sauce is to first make a roux by slowly cooking flour and butter (or oil) together. The color range of roux is shown on the **back cover** of this book. If your roux is going to be dark, then you must use either oil or clarified butter to avoid it being bitter because the milk solids in butter burn on prolonged heating. Always cook the roux slowly in a nonreactive vessel (do not use aluminum, copper or cast iron) for best results. Attempting to cook roux quickly on a higher heat will result in both bitterness and less thickening power, as explained in previous volumes.

True classic Béchamel involves simmering the white sauce with a pique (an onion studded with cloves and bay leaf) and seasoning it with a little white pepper and nutmeg. These refinements are unnecessary in most of today's applications with bold flavors. You won't taste the difference unless your dish is very bland, as was often the case in Old World cuisine.

PICCATA PAN SAUCE

Piccata does not usually have green olives in it, but this will add more complexity for imitation meat dishes. Also, even people who hate green olives will not notice them in this sauce from what I have seen over the years.

30g (1 oz)	Butter
15g (0.5 oz)	Garlic, minced
25g (0.9 oz)	Shallots, minced
25g (0.9 oz)	Green Olives
15g (0.5 oz)	Capers
30ml (1 oz)	Lemon Juice, fresh
1 T	Parsley, freshly minced

PROCEDURE

1. Rinse the capers quickly under running water. Put them out on a cutting board with the green olives and roughly chop them with a chef's knife until no large pieces remain.

2. Heat the butter in a nonstick skillet on medium (#6 out of 10). You can use the same pan you browned the faux fish fillets in, if this is for that application.

3. When the butter has foamed up, add the garlic and shallots. Cook for about 2 minutes with occasional stirring.

4. Now add the green olives and capers. Lower the heat slightly and cook for another 1-2 minutes.

5. Add the lemon juice and parsley. Cook for about 30 seconds.

6. Take the pan off the heat and continue stirring for another 30 seconds. This is now ready to use, or you can mix with a little mayonnaise, too.

MUSHROOM GRAVY

Normally mushroom gravies are made with beef or veal stock, but this one delivers on flavor without any meat at all.

100g (3.5 oz)	Mushrooms
60ml (2 oz)	Olive Oil (in all)
30g (1 oz)	Flour
20g (0.8 oz)	Shallots, chopped
1 clove	Garlic, peeled and cut in thirds
1 teaspoon	Deep Undertones Spice (page 142)
1/4 teaspoon	Rosemary, dried
1/4 teaspoon	Thyme, dried
1/4 teaspoon	Black Pepper, ground
125ml (4.4 oz)	Cream
125ml (4.4 oz)	Milk
1/2 teaspoon	Mediterranean Meat Spice (page 142)
1/4 teaspoon	White Pepper, finely ground
3-4 whole	Sage leaves, fresh (optional)

ADDITIONAL INFORMATION

At step #10 in the cooking procedure, you add water. If you are not strictly vegetarian, an even better result will be obtained if you add chicken or beef broth. Do not add vegetable stock, though.

PROCEDURE

1. Cut the mushrooms into large pieces. If they are small mushrooms, then this step is not necessary.
2. Heat a saucepan on a medium-high (#7 out of 10) heat. When it is hot, add 15ml (1 tablespoon) of the olive oil to the pan. Wait a minute for the oil to get to temperature and then add the mushrooms. Fry them for 5 minutes until they are golden.
3. Remove the mushrooms to a bowl using a slotted spoon.

4. Remove the pan from the heat and add the rest of the olive oil. Wait for about 2 full minutes.

5. Add the flour to the oil (off the heat still) and stir constantly for the next minute or so. The cold oil and flour will reduce the heat at the bottom of the pan. Scrape to pick up the fond from the mushrooms during this time.

6. Now put the pan on a medium-low heat (#4 out of 10) and continue stirring frequently for quite a while. You are going to make a BROWN roux (see **back cover**).

7. By now the mushrooms should have cooled off. Drain the liquid that ran off of them back into the roux. Cut each mushroom piece in half.

8. Add the mushrooms to the brown roux along with the shallots and the clove of garlic. Cook with occasional stirring for about 5 minutes.

9. Grind the thyme, rosemary and black pepper in a mortar to obtain a powder.

10. Add the cream, milk, Deep Undertones Spice and the powdered thyme, rosemary and black pepper. Stir while you bring it to a simmer. Maintain at a simmer until it is thick.

11. Add 100ml (3.5 oz) water and stir.

12. Transfer contents to a blender and purée.

13. Rub blended purée through a mesh sieve. Discard solids.

14. Rinse out the pan that was previously used, then add the sieved sauce back. Return to a low heat. Add the Midrange Mediterranean Meat Spice, the white pepper and the sage leaves (if you are using them).

15. Simmer for 5-10 minutes.

16. Remove the sage leaves and transfer the rest to a bowl to cool. Taste and adjust salt level.

AURORA SAUCE

This isn't exactly the classic Sauce Aurore, but it is very similar and designed to function in the recipes here. The name means sunrise because of its color. In many instances in this book, it is used in place of simple Béchamel because it has a deeper and richer flavor, but the same thickening properties.

30ml (1 oz)	Vegetable Oil
30g (1 oz)	Flour
30g (1 oz)	Onion, single large piece
50g (1.75 oz)	Tomato Purée (passata)
150ml (5.3 oz)	* Vegetable Broth (page 119)
150ml (5,3 oz)	Milk (not lowfat)
4 whole	Cloves (the spice)
1 whole	Bay Leaf
1/2 teaspoon	Salt
1/4 teaspoon	Black Pepper, ground

THE PIQUE

A *pique* is an onion that has been studded with cloves. Classic Béchamel Sauce is simmered with a pique in it, but I rarely bother with that because today's foods have more intense flavors that overshadow the subtle difference you would taste in classic French haute cuisine, sometimes in which Béchamel sauce was the dominant flavor. A perfect example is, *Poisson Cuit Dans Béchamel* (fish baked in Béchamel sauce). Obviously the details of the Béchamel are of paramount importance if it is the only flavoring. Conversely, if the Béchamel is a glaze over a spicy burrito to provide color and richness after it's flashed under a broiler, there is no point in bothering with delicately flavoring the Béchamel. With vegetable dishes that need more flavor, Aurora Sauce is treated like enhanced Béchamel. It is a bit more work, but well worth it here.

PROCEDURE

1. Pour the oil into a saucepan on a medium-high heat (#7 out of 10).

2. When it is hot (just over 100°C / 210°F) then add the flour and stir. Reduce the heat to medium (#5 out of 10).

3. Continue stirring with a nonreactive spoon (wood is traditional, but silicone is fine) until the roux reaches the CHESTNUT stage (see **back cover**).

4. During this time, prepare the *pique* by pushing the cloves into the onion, using two of them to "nail" the bay leaf to the onion, as well.

5. When the roux has reached the right color, add the tomato purée and increase the heat back to medium-high (#7 out of 10). Stir constantly.

6. The mixture will tighten to become like a loose dough. As soon as it reaches this stage, begin counting the time. Fry this mixture for about 2 minutes, stirring frequently.

7. Now add the vegetable broth and use a wire whisk to dissolve the roux into the stock.

8. Add the milk, salt and black pepper. Whisk to make smooth.

9. Bring to a slow simmer, then reduce the heat to medium-low (#4 out of

10. Now add the onion pique you prepared. Make sure the clove/bay side is facing down in the pot.

11. Maintain at a slow simmer with occasional stirring for 20 minutes. You will see red dots appear on the surface during this time, and the mixture will gradually become more orange in color, as well as much thicker. Adjust heat to keep it from actually boiling,or the opposite - just steaming. You want small bubbles to be breaking the surface. Finally, be sure to scrape the sides of the vessel so that you don't end up with any uncooked roux in the final sauce.

* Note that if you are not a strict vegetarian, you can substitute chicken stock for the vegetable stock in this recipe.

✦

GREEK SAUCE

As a tofu marinade or an outstanding Greek salad dressing.

200g (7 oz)	Tomatoes, fresh
30g (1 oz)	Cucumber, fresh
30g (1 oz)	Olive Oil, extra virgin
25g (0.9 oz)	Feta cheese, mild cow milk type
15g (0.5 oz)	Scallions
15g (0.5 oz)	Parsley, fresh
1 T	Lime Juice, fresh
1/2 teaspoon	Mustard, prepared
1/2 teaspoon	Balsamic Vinegar

PROCEDURE

1. Slice the round ends off of the tomatoes and discard them. Cut the rest into 6cm (1/4 inch) slices.

2. Preheat the oven to 200°C (390°F) and position a shelf 12cm (5 inches) from the heating element.

3. Lay the tomato slices in a single layer on a Silpat (silicone mat) on a baking tray. Sprinkle with salt. Change the oven setting to broil. Place the tray of tomato slices under the broiler for about 15 minutes until they are blackened at the edges and quite shriveled up, but not really burnt.

4. Scrape the tomatoes from the mat into the cup of a stick blender. Add to this all of the other ingredients except only for the Balsamic vinegar. Purée until homogeneous.

5. Rub through a sieve. This is going to take a few minutes to get as much as possible (some can't pass because of the skin of the tomatoes and other fibrous plant matter, but get what you can through

6. Add the Balsamic vinegar. Add salt to taste. This has a very long shelf life in the refrigerator.

DEMI-GLACE REPLACEMENT

Provides thickening and some similar background notes for use in sauces and other preparations.

400ml (14 oz)	Vegetable Broth (page 119)
22g (0.5 oz)	Olive Oil
2 T	Flour
15g (0.5 oz)	Garlic cloves, peeled
1/2 teaspoon	Deep Undertones Spice (page 142)
1-2 sprigs	Parsley, fresh
1 whole	Bay Leaf, dried Turkish
4-6 whole	White Peppercorns

PROCEDURE

1. Heat a sauce pan on a medium setting (#5 out of 10). When it is quite warm (but not blazing hot) add the olive oil. Wait 30 seconds.

2. Add the flour and stir almost constantly. Cook until the roux is at the TOASTY stage (see **back cover**).

3. Reduce heat to low (#3 out of 10). Cut each clove of garlic into four pieces. Add this to the roux and stir. Cook until the garlic is starting to brown, but not burn.

4. Add all of the other ingredients and increase the heat back to medium. Stir to combine and cook for about 15 minutes, counting time from after it comes to a simmer. Maintain as close to 77°C (170°F) as possible.

5. Rub through a sieve. You should have about 150 grams (5.3 oz) of finished product. If it is much more, then return it to the stove to gently reduce further (add the solids from the sieve back in and repeat this step after it has reduced. If there is a little less, then add water. If it is less than 100 grams, then you burned it.

TOMATO SUGO & ESPAGNOLE

The Tomato Sugo here is more complex than the standard Italian preparation, but if you want vegetarian cuisine to be as satisfying and rich as meat dishes, you have to bring more layers of flavor. The Espagnole is surprisingly similar to the classic, considering that this contains no veal or any other meat.

350g (12.3 oz)	Tomato Purée (passata)
150g (5.3 oz)	Tomatoes, fresh
100g (3.5 oz)	Onions, diced small
60g (2 oz)	Celery, diced small
60g (2 oz)	Carrots, diced small
30g (1 oz)	Butter
25ml (0.9 oz)	Olive Oil
15ml (0.5 oz)	Cognac or Brandy
1 T	Flour
2 whole	Garlic cloves, peeled
1 whole	Bay Leaf
1 1/2 teaspoons	Mediterranean Meat Spice (page 142)
1 teaspoon	Maggi Seasoning
1 teaspoon	Salt
3/4 teaspoon	Paprika
1/2 teaspoon	Thyme, dried
6-8 whole	Basil leaves, fresh

PROCEDURE

1. Cut the tomato into large pieces so that there is a fairly flat surface with skin. This is the same cut shown in the Italian Tomato Paste video.

2. Select a nonreactive saucepan about 2 liters in size. Heat this on high (#8 out of 10). When it is hot, add the olive oil and swirl to distribute it.

3. Add the cut tomato pieces. Position so that they are skin-side down. Cook for about 6 minutes. There should be blistering and some browning on the skin side.

4. Add the diced onion, celery and carrot. Also add the paprika. Stir occasionally, leaving the heat on high. Cook for about 10 minutes.

5. Reduce heat slightly (#7) and add the salt and bay leaf. Smash the garlic cloves with the side of a knife and add those to the pan, too. Cook for about 3 more minutes with frequent stirring.

6. Add the tomato purée (passata) and the flour. Stir together well as you bring it to a simmer.

7. Reduce heat to medium (#5 out of 10) and cover. Ideally use a lid that has a small hole in the top to vent steam. Cook for 1 hour and 15 minutes, stirring about every 15 minutes. Adjust heat to maintain at a simmer, as necessary.

8. Add 200ml (7 oz) of water. Stir and then scrape into a blender. Also addd the basil leaves, the thyme, the cognac, the Maggi Seasoning and the Mediterranean Meat Spice to the blender. Purée.

9. Wipe out the pan that had been used for cooking it. Rub the puréed mixture through a sieve back into the pan. Discard the solids collected in the sieve. Put a splatter guard over the pan and bring to a simmer. There will be a lot of splattering and popping. Give it a quick stir about every 5 minutes. Simmer for 15-20 minutes in all. The splattering should have subsided by the end of this cooking time.

10. Add the butter and turn the heat off, but leave the pan on the burner. Stir to incorporate the butter as it melts into the sauce. Add a couple of twists of freshly ground black pepper.

11. Transfer to a bowl to cool down at room temperature for a while before refrigerating or freezing. You should have about 400 grams (14 ounces) of product at this point. **This is the Tomato Sugo.**

ESPAGNOLE SUBSTITUTE

Stir together equal portions by weight of the Tomato Sugu with the Demi-glace Replacement (page 135). Simmer for 15 minutes.

VODKA CHILI ELIXIR

Although this can be used as a hot sauce almost directly (see directions at the end of this recipe), the best application is if you add this to other ingredients, which can be as simple as ketchup or mayonnaise. This mixture is rich in polyphenols, which affect our perception of flavors more than being flavors themselves. This is explained in detail in Volume 3.

100g (3.5 oz)	Red Chilies (see note below)
60ml (2.1 oz)	Rice Wine Vinegar
28g (1 oz)	Garlic cloves, peeled
30ml + 1 T (1.5 oz)	Vodka (in all)
28g (1 oz)	Sugar
1 teaspoon	Salt
100ml (3.5 oz)	Water (see note below)

ADDITIONAL INFORMATION

If at all possible, use ripe (red) New Mexico or Hatch chilies for this. You can substitute other varieties, but the flavor and amount of heat will vary accordingly, of course. Don't use Jalapeño or Thai chilies because their flavor profiles are incompatible. Serrano chilies are okay, but not the best here.

Also, for best results you want to use mineral water for this and not ordinary tap water. I use *Borjomi* for this, but you can use *Perrier*, which is more widely available.

PROCEDURE

1. Trim off the stems from the chilies, then cut them into large pieces.
2. Heat a stainless steel pan (do <u>not</u> use nonstick or cast iron) on a high heat (#8 out of 10) until it is smoking hot.

3. Add the chilies to the pan. Stir only occasionally. You want to achieve a blistered and partly blackened surface on them. This will take 4 to 5 minutes.

4. During this time, chop the garlic up. This will give it time to react in the air and develop its pungent aroma.

5. When the chilies are well blistered, turn the heat off, but continue to cook with occasional stirring for another 2-3 minutes as the pan cools and the residual heat subsides.

6. Now add the water followed by 30ml (1 oz) of the vodka). Stir and scrape the bottom of the pan to deglaze it. Continue about 2 minutes.

7. Transfer the contents to the cup of a stick blender, or to a regular blender if you are scaling this up. Add the rice wine vinegar, the garlic, the sugar and the salt. Purée.

8. Rinse and wipe out the pan you used to blister the chilies. Put it back on the stove and add the mixture from the blender.

9. Bring to a simmer, stirring occasionally. Maintain at a simmer for about 8 minutes until the mixture is thickened. If you have scaled up this recipe it will take longer.

10. Transfer the contents to a food mill equipped with the medium perforated plate. You cannot use a sieve for this. It will take a little work to get most of it through, and remember to scrape the bottom of the food mill to get all of the sauce through.

11. Now add the last tablespoon of vodka to the sauce. Put it in a sealed container and refrigerate. It is best after it sits in the refrigerator for a couple of days, and it will keep for a very long time as long as it is cold.

VODKA CHILI HOT SAUCE

You can make an intriguing hot sauce just by combing the Vodka Chili Elixir with distilled white vinegar to taste. The ratio will be about 3 to 4 parts of Vodka Chili Elixir to 1 to 2 parts vinegar.

Spice Blends

Although the blending of spices is important in almost every notable dish, these particular mixes comprise an essential arsenal for creating meat-like flavors. Most of the ingredients are easily found, except dried Thai basil, which is used in two of the key blends, and is much better than regular basil for these recipes. You can dry your own if you find get the fresh for sale.

HIDDEN SALAMI SPICE

As part of a dish, this suggests the familiar flavor of cured sausage.

1 1/2 teaspoons	Smoked Paprika (Pimentón)
1 1/2 teaspoons	Fennel Seeds, whole
1 teaspoon	Black Peppercorns, whole
1 teaspoon	Sage, dried
1 teaspoon	Cumin seeds, whole
1 teaspoon	Coarse Salt
1 teaspoon	Dark Brown Sugar, ideally Muscovado
1/2 teaspoon	Garlic Powder
1/2 teaspoon	Coffee, instant
1/8 to 1/2 teaspoon	Cayenne, ground (see note below)

The amount of cayenne is subject to taste. If you are sensitive to spicy foods, then use the minimum. If you want it to have a little kick, as many types of salami do, then add more. Don't go beyond half a teaspoon or the balance will be off..

Grind all of the ingredients together in an electric spice mill.

141

DEEP UNDERTONES SPICE BLEND

This simulates some of the very deep flavors produced by the Maillard reaction at the point close to pyrolysis.

1 T	Cumin seeds
2 teaspoons	Coarse Salt
1 3/4 teaspoons	Coffee, instant
1 1/2 teaspoons	Basil, dried (ideally Thai Basil)
1 1/4 teaspoons	Mustard, dry
1 teaspoon	Black Peppercorns, whole
3/4 teaspoon	Sage, dried
1/2 teaspoon	Paprika
1/4 teaspoon	Coriander Seeds

Grind all of the ingredients together to a powder in an electric spice mill. As with other ground spices, the shelf life is limited.

MEDITERRANEAN MEAT SPICE

This simple blend adds mid-range meat tones and is especially compatible with Italian flavors and ingredients. It packs some heat, too.

1 T	MSG
1-2 whole	Dried Red Chilies (see note below)
2 teaspoons	Basil, dried (ideally Thai Basil)
1 teaspoon	Chives, dried
1 teaspoon	Black Peppercorns, whole
1 teaspoon	Coarse Salt
3/4 teaspoon	Garlic Powder
1/4 teaspoon	Sugar, brown

If the chilies are small, then use two. Drying chilies is described in detail in *Cooking in Russia, Volume 1*. Simply grind all of the ingredients together in an electric spice mill.

TONKATSU TOFU SPICE BLEND

To produce the spice blend, simply combine all of the following ingredients in an electric spice mill and grind to a powder.

2 teaspoons	White Peppercorns
1 1/2 teaspoons	Thyme, dried
1 teaspoon	Coarse Salt
1 teaspoon	Rosemary, dried
1 teaspoon	Brown Sugar, ideally Muscovado
1/2 teaspoon	Black Peppercorns
1/2 teaspoon	Garlic Powder
1/2 teaspoon	MSG
1/4 teaspoon	Turmeric

Store in a sealed jar away from direct light. Best used within a month, but still useable after two months.

TONKATSU MARINADE & COOKING DIRECTIONS

Purée the following in the cup of a stick blender. Multiply to scale up.

1 T	Chicken Spice Blend (see above)
25g (0.9 oz)	Shallots, chopped
40ml (1.4 oz)	Water
10ml (0.3 oz)	Rice Vinegar

Press 6 tofu strips, each about 10x1.5x1.5cm (4"x1/2"x1/2") between sheets of paper towel to absorb as much water as possible. Then marinate the strips for 1-3 hours, turning occasionally. Prepare a breading station with flour in the first container. The second container is a mixture of one egg, one teaspoon baking powder (not baking soda), one tablespoon milk and 1/2 teaspoon salt. The third container is panko or coarse bread crumbs. After coating, set them aside to rest for 15 minutes while you heat oil for deep frying to 170°C (350°F). Fry for just over 2 minutes, then dust with a pinch of the same Tonkatsu Spice Blend shown at the top of this page.

Index

145

U

V

W, X, Y, Z

CPSIA information can be obtained
at www.ICGtesting.com
Printed in the USA
BVHW081217280820
587369BV00002B/163